When Worldviews Collide

Christians Confronting Culture

Ergun Mehmet Caner

Learning Activities by Dale McCleskey

LifeWay Press®
Nashville, Tennessee

Published by LifeWay Press®
© 2005 Ergun Mehmet Caner
Fourth printing 2007

ISBN 1-4158-2114-3
Item 001274629

This book is the resource for course CG-1088 in the Ministry category
of the Christian Growth Study Plan.

Dewey decimal classification: 261.2
Subject headings: CHRISTIANITY AND OTHER RELIGIONS \
CHURCH AND SOCIAL PROBLEMS \ CHRISTIAN SOCIOLOGY

Unless otherwise noted, all Scripture quotations are taken from
the Holman Christian Standard Bible®, copyright © 1999, 2000, 2002, 2003
by Holman Bible Publishers. Used by permission. Scripture quotations marked NIV
are taken from the Holy Bible, New International Version, copyright © 1973, 1978, 1984
by International Bible Society. Scripture quotations marked NASB are taken from
New American Standard Bible®, Copyright © 1960, 1962, 1963, 1968, 1971, 1972, 1973,
1975, 1977, 1995 by the Lockman Foundation. Used by permission. *(www.lockman.org)*

Selected doctrinal responses and witnessing tips are adapted
from *FAITH Discipleship: Faith Reaching Out to World Religions,*
© 2001 LifeWay Press® (out of print). For information about FAITH Evangelism®,
phone toll free (877) 324-8498 or visit *www.lifeway.com/faith.*

To order additional copies of this resource, write to LifeWay Church Resources Customer Service;
One LifeWay Plaza; Nashville, TN 37234-0113; fax (615) 251-5933; phone toll free (800) 458-2772;
e-mail *orderentry@lifeway.com;* order online at *www.lifeway.com;*
or visit the LifeWay Christian Store serving you.

Printed in the United States of America

Leadership and Adult Publishing
LifeWay Church Resources
One LifeWay Plaza
Nashville, TN 37234-0175

Contents

About the Author

Ergun Mehmet Caner (Th.M., Southeastern Seminary; Th.D., University of South Africa) is the dean of Liberty Baptist Theological Seminary and a professor of theology and church history at Liberty University in Lynchburg, Virginia. Elected dean in February 2005, Dr. Caner is the first former Muslim to become a dean of an evangelical seminary. His specific area of expertise is world religions and the world of global apologetics.

Along with his brother, Emir (a professor of history and a dean at Southwestern Baptist Theological Seminary), Ergun is the author of 11 books, including the best-seller *Christian Jihad* (Kregel, 2004), which examines the recent war in light of 1,300 years of Islamic-Christian conflict. In 2003 his book *Unveiling Islam* won the Gold Medallion Award from the Evangelical Christian Publishers Association.

In the war on terror, Caner understands both sides because he has been on both sides. He was reared the son of an Islamic leader. In 1982 he converted to the Christian faith after immigrating to this country. As a consequence of this conversion, he was disowned by his family.

Since the September 11 attacks, Caner has appeared on such national television shows as *Fox News*, various CNN broadcasts, MSNBC, *The 700 Club*, Zola Levitt, John Ankerberg, and others.

Caner and his wife, Jill, have two sons.

While Caner's message in *When Worldviews Collide* is cutting edge, it is also personal and warm. As a former pastor, he illuminates challenging issues and questions with truths from God's Word, especially from the Apostle Paul's experiences with the early church. Throughout this eight-week study Caner reminds us that the harvest is great: "*When Worldviews Collide* brings evangelism into the global market, taking apologetics to a world of 4.8 billion people. If we were to live one hundred years, we would never be able to see the complete fruit of this work."

About the Study

The world has come to us. No longer a homogeneous Christian nation, our land is the home of millions of Hindus, Buddhists, Jews, Muslims, spiritualists, and atheists. Our culture constantly admonishes Christians to compromise our beliefs and exercise tolerance for belief systems that deny the truth of Jesus Christ and God's written Word. How should you as a believer respond to today's climate of religious diversity? Is it even possible to understand the beliefs and assumptions of these faiths? How can we share the good news of salvation with those who follow other belief systems?

When Worldviews Collide can equip you to confront your culture with truth and compassion. After completing this eight-week, interactive study, you will be able to—

- identify six ways Christianity differs from other belief systems;
- summarize the basic beliefs of four major world religions (Hinduism, Buddhism, Judaism, and Islam) and several prevalent cultural philosophies;
- state biblical responses to non-Christian beliefs;
- identify ways to minister and witness to followers of other belief systems.

The Bible-study framework for this course is the Book of Acts, especially the Apostle Paul's defenses of Christianity. Review the contents page (3) to get an idea of what you will be studying. You're in for a life-changing ride!

This study consists of eight group sessions. After the introductory session, in which you will hear Ergun Caner's dramatic conversion story, your group will follow this format in the seven remaining group sessions:

1. *Greeting and prayer.*
2. *Review.* On DVD the author reviews the material you studied during the previous week in your member book.
3. *Group discussion.* Your leader will guide the discussion and help you make appropriate applications to your life.
4. *DVD teaching segment.* The author previews the subject of the next week's study in the member book.
5. *Closure*

Make a commitment to other members in your group to attend faithfully and to participate meaningfully. Prayerfully prepare and fully participate in the discussion and group activities. Use this experience to strengthen your relationships and your walk with the Lord, as well as to confront your culture as Christ would do.

This member book provides content for the study as well as activities to help you learn and apply the material. Completing home study between sessions will greatly enhance your learning experience. You can expect to spend about 30 minutes each day as you complete five days of home study each week. Your member book also includes video viewer guides that you will complete as you watch corresponding DVD segments during the group sessions.

Leader help is available for facilitating a group study. *When Worldviews Collide: Christians Confronting Culture Leader DVD and CD-ROM* (ISBN 1-4158-2297-2) includes these items:

Leader Guide. The session plans in this leader guide provide step-by-step suggestions for planning and conducting eight group sessions.

Leader supplements. The CD-ROM provides leader supplements for additional study. These supplements are not required for the course, but they include additional statistics and articles that will equip the leader to lead from an overflow of knowledge and to answer questions. Copies may be made for group members as needed.

Session handouts. The CD-ROM also provides handouts for use during the sessions. The leader guide provides directions for using the handouts.

DVDs. Two DVDs feature the author, Ergun Caner, teaching the content of each session's study and reviewing the previous week's study in the member book. The DVDs also provide a church promotional segment; "A Word to the Pastor"; "From Ergun Caner's Heart"; and "In Their Own Words," multiple bonus segments featuring interviews with followers of non-Christian belief systems.

Depending on the amount of time your group has available, optional bonus interviews can provide information about followers of other faiths in their own words. Longer interviews with a spiritualist, Hindu, Buddhist, Messianic Jew, and Islamic *imam* may be used as the leader chooses and as the group desires.

Shorter segments of each interview are also provided and are suggested for optional use in appropriate sessions. These uses are described on the *Leader DVD and CD-ROM* cover.

For example, after hearing the author's presentation on Hinduism, studying it during the week, and briefly reviewing it at the next group session, some groups may want to see the interview with Aruna, the young woman who practices Hinduism. Many of her thoughts will confirm what they have learned elsewhere and will add a contemporary flavor to the study.

You will often hear this thought from Dr. Caner in this study: "God commanded us to go into all the world. To some extent we did not, so He has brought the world to us. Our responsibilities and opportunities are great, and we must be prepared." As you begin this study, ask God to speak to you about ways you can grow as a witness for Christ and as an apologist for biblical truth. You will find yourself observing current events from a new perspective, and you will develop a heart of compassion for followers of other faiths.

Viewer Guide
Introductory Group Session

We will examine four major world religions:

1. _____   2. _____   3. _____   4. _____

Two types of Muslims:

1. _____ Muslims   2. _____ Muslims

Devout Muslims observe the Five Pillars of Islam.

Every Muslim lives and dies by the _____.

There is only one eternal assurance in Islam; only one thing erases bad scales—
to die as a _____.

Jesus _____ so that I wouldn't have to.

_____ _____ people espouse the beliefs we will study in coming weeks.

God said "Go to all the world and preach the gospel to every creature."
We didn't. So He brought the world here, to your _____.

Our study is not about gathering _____. It's about gathering _____.
Our study is about broken _____ more than golden _____.

Teaching Segment: Six Degrees of Separation

Christianity is not a _____. It is a relationship with God.

Six degrees of separation distinguish Christianity from other belief systems:
1. Only Christianity refers to God as _____.
2. Only in Christianity do you have a God who has an _____
   _____ with you.
3. Only in Christianity is Jesus Christ not only Teacher but also _____.
4. Only in Christianity does God operate by _____.
5. Only in Christianity is everyone _____ before the cross.
6. Only in Christianity does God accept you _____ _____ _____.

See them the way Christ sees them: someone for whom He _____.
The God who _____ us wants to _____ them as well.

1 Six Degrees of Separation

What Differentiates Christianity from the World's Religions?

Agrippa said to Paul, "It is permitted for you to speak for yourself."

Then Paul stretched out his hand and began his defense: "I consider myself fortunate, King Agrippa, that today I am going to make a defense before you about everything I am accused of by the Jews, especially since you are an expert in all the Jewish customs and controversies. Therefore I beg you to listen to me patiently.

"All the Jews know my way of life from my youth, which was spent from the beginning among my own nation and in Jerusalem. They had previously known me for quite some time, if they were willing to testify, that according to the strictest party of our religion I lived as

GLOBAL SNAPSHOT

- Most surveys show there are more than one billion Christians on the earth, but this includes many who are not believers in Christ alone as Lord.
- Christianity is not a religion in that it does not offer people a way to approach God. In Christianity God approaches humanity.

THIS WEEK'S GOAL

No.1

After this week's study you will be able to—

- identify six beliefs that separate Christianity from other systems;
- state implications of the belief that God is Father;
- explain why it is impossible to separate Christ from Christianity and why the resurrection is pivotal;
- identify the role of grace in salvation and in the Christian life;
- state why the world is our mission field.

a Pharisee. And now I stand on trial for the hope of the promise made by God to our fathers, the promise our 12 tribes hope to attain as they earnestly serve Him night and day. Because of this hope I am being accused by the Jews, O king! Why is it considered incredible by any of you that God raises the dead? In fact, I myself supposed it was necessary to do many things in opposition to the name of Jesus the Nazarene. This I actually did in Jerusalem, and I locked up many of the saints in prison, since I had received authority for that from the chief priests. When they were put to death, I cast my vote against them. In all the synagogues I often tried to make them blaspheme by punishing them. Being greatly enraged at them, I even pursued them to foreign cities.

"Under these circumstances I was traveling to Damascus with authority and a commission from the chief priests. At midday, while on the road, O king, I saw a light from heaven brighter than the sun, shining around me and those traveling with me. When we had all fallen to the ground, I heard a voice speaking to me in the Hebrew language, 'Saul, Saul, why are you persecuting Me? It is hard for you to kick against the goads.'

"But I said, 'Who are You, Lord?'

"And the Lord replied: 'I am Jesus, whom you are persecuting. But get up and stand on your feet. For I have appeared to you for this purpose, to appoint you as a servant and a witness of things you have seen, and of things in which I will appear to you. I will rescue you from the people and from the Gentiles, to whom I now send you, to open their eyes that they may turn from darkness to light and from the power of Satan to God, that they may receive forgiveness of sins and a share among those who are sanctified by faith in Me.'

"Therefore, King Agrippa, I was not disobedient to the heavenly vision. Instead, I preached to those in Damascus first, and to those in Jerusalem and in all the region of Judea, and to the Gentiles, that they should repent and turn to God, and do works worthy of repentance. For this reason the Jews seized me in the temple complex and were trying to kill me. Since I have obtained help that comes from God, to this day I stand and testify to both small and great, saying nothing else than what the prophets and Moses said would take place—that the Messiah must suffer, and that as the first to rise from the dead, He would proclaim light to our people and to the Gentiles."

Acts 26:1-23

Are You Religious?

In light of today's prevalent notion that all religions are created equal, this passage raises some interesting questions: Why would Paul have endangered his life and endured persecution if all religions are the same? Was he a natural fighter? Was he just a sectarian and a racist who needed an enemy? Or was the gospel of Jesus so radically different and exclusive that Paul willingly faced death to preach Christ?

How do you think Paul would be treated today in our culture? Would he be castigated for being narrow-minded? Would he be seen as a self-loathing Jew who was now committed to persecuting his own people? Would other religious groups rise up as self-proclaimed victims and assert that Paul was guilty of hate speech?

In his brief ministry, from his first missionary journey in A.D. 48 until his martyrdom by Nero in A.D. 68, Paul was hunted, hounded, stoned, threatened, tried, whipped, and imprisoned. He wrote 14 books, started churches on two continents, and preached in a myriad of cities. He addressed murderous barbarians in Crete and the philosophical elite in Athens. He stood before governors, councils, and King Agrippa. He was imprisoned twice in Rome, once under a type of house arrest and then in a dungeon on death row.

In this passage Paul gave the Corinthian church a moving summary of his life as a witness for Christ:

> *[I have suffered] far more labors, many more imprisonments, far worse beatings, [and was] near death many times. Five times I received from the Jews 40 lashes minus one. Three times I was beaten with rods. Once I was stoned. Three times I was shipwrecked. I have spent a night and a day in the depths of the sea. On frequent journeys, I faced dangers from rivers, dangers from robbers, dangers from my own people, dangers from the Gentiles, dangers in the city, dangers in the open country, dangers on the sea, and dangers among false brothers; labor and hardship, many sleepless nights, hunger and thirst, often without food, cold, and lacking clothing. Not to mention other things, there is the daily pressure on me: my care for all the churches.*
> 2 Corinthians 11:23-28

Quite a ministry résumé, isn't it? Would it not have been easier for Paul to let religious people in the various belief systems remain religious? If Paul had just made a few appearances and complimented the religious groups for their sincerity, he would have become a respected leader in the community.

Yet Paul knew a secret: *Christianity is not a religion.*

Read that again. It is not a misprint. It is a central precept of Christianity.

Christianity is not a movement of ethical prescriptions or philosophical beliefs that mark humanity's search for God. The core essentials that compose our faith are marked by clear distinctions that segregate us from the rest of the world. This week you will examine those six degrees of separation.

One of those differences drives us back into the world. We are called to reach every single breathing soul on the planet. It is our call and our life. As you study this week, focus not only on the doctrinal differences but also on the central command of the One who is our Redeemer: " 'Go, therefore, and make disciples of all nations, baptizing them in the name of the Father and of the Son and of the Holy Spirit, teaching them to observe everything I have commanded you' " (Matt. 28:19-20).

Christ did not call us to conquer the lost. Christ called us to win them to Him.

Day 1: God Is Father

As Paul stood before King Agrippa, he faced not only the indictment of a political world but also the skepticism of an unbelieving religious world. He had already addressed philosophers in Athens, and it had been clear that his listeners did not recognize the God he was preaching (see Acts 17). Yet his message never changed. Paul had also given other clear sermons and defenses on his way to Rome:

- Paul had given a farewell sermon to the leaders of the Ephesian church (see Acts 20:17-35), where he spoke of the Lord Jesus and the Holy Spirit (see vv. 21,23).
- Paul had addressed an unruly crowd in Jerusalem, as well as the Council there (see Acts 22:1-21; 23:1-10).
- When Paul arrived in Caesarea, he had preached to the governor, Felix (see Acts 24:10-21).

Now Paul stood before the king, who was visiting the governor. In Acts 26:6 Paul summarized the indictment against him: " 'I stand on trial for the hope of the promise made by God to our fathers.' " Who was this God Paul preached? It was the Lord who directly addressed him: " 'When we had all fallen to the ground, I heard a voice speaking to me in the Hebrew language, "Saul, Saul, why are you persecuting Me? It is hard for you to kick against the goads." But I said, "Who are You, Lord?" And the Lord replied: "I am Jesus, whom you are persecuting" ' " (Acts 26:14-15).

Did Paul misspeak? Surely he did not mean that he was speaking directly with God (*theos*) and the Lord (*kurios*), did he? And surely he did not mean to call Jesus Lord, did he?

Yes, he did.

Paul was illustrating the first clear point of demarcation between Christianity and every major world religion:

World religions speak of a God who is judge.
Christianity preaches a God who is Father.

No other system except Christianity speaks of an intimate, personal relationship between the Creator and humans. Hinduism teaches an impersonal litany of gods who are removed from the earthly plane. The belief system of Buddhism denies a personal being. Islam offers a god who is judge and creator. But no other belief system speaks of God in intimate terms.

Read Romans 8:14-18 in the margin and underline the terms of intimacy.

Did you notice the intimacy with which we approach God? The primary distinctive is found in the term *Father.* The concept of God as Father is profoundly different from that of all other religions, and it speaks volumes about His nature and His relationship with humanity.

"All those led by God's Spirit are God's sons. For you did not receive a spirit of slavery to fall back into fear, but you received the Spirit of adoption, by whom we cry out, 'Abba, Father!' The Spirit Himself testifies together with our spirit that we are God's children, and if children, also heirs— heirs of God and co-heirs with Christ—seeing that we suffer with Him so that we may also be glorified with Him. For I consider that the sufferings of this present time are not worth comparing with the glory that is going to be revealed to us."
Romans 8:14-18

At what point do you first remember hearing or realizing that God is Father?

_____

What practical difference does viewing God as Father mean to you?

_____

_____

The Romans passage also tells us that the Holy Spirit testifies that we are God's children. Islam calls this idea blasphemy. Other systems call this teaching futile. Yet Christianity hinges on the central tenet that we enter a relationship with God that transcends a Judge-penitent relationship. Once born again, we become His children.

The inference here is a great insight. God deals with us lovingly, as a father to his children. As our divine Parent, He intercedes in our lives from His love for us. This love surpasses any other type of relationship. He is Father. Consider that:

> *In your darkest hour the Father soothes your sorrow.*
> *In your worst pain the Father is the Balm who heals.*
> *In your secret anxiety the Father calms your fear.*
> *In your brokenness the Father comforts your heart.*

The average person on the street would be bewildered by your prayer life. Why, they would ask, if there is a God, would He be concerned about your pitiful little life? In a world consumed by hunger, disease, disaster, and war, why would God care about one person's problems? Such a claim seems somewhat narcissistic, does it not?

How would you answer the objection that God doesn't have time for your problems?

_____

Is it too much to expect God to care about us? Not if He is Father!

On any given day I deal with a myriad of phone calls, messages, letters, and appointments. Because we have been on the frontlines of the Christian-Islamic debate in the media, my office receives about 40 inquiries a day from around the world. As the dean of a seminary, I have many responsibilities that often keep me sequestered in my office until well past dark. Add to that my teaching responsibilities, the speaking, the travel, and the writing, and I feel that I have more on my plate than I can fathom. Maybe you can relate to this schedule!

Yet my entire world pauses when my son Braxton calls. Regardless of where I am or what I am doing, I stop it all and attend to him. It will be the same when Drake gets a bit older as well.

Why would my sons' concerns take priority? Because I am their father. Regardless of whatever the world may call me, no word carries as much inherent purpose as *father*. It is a man's highest calling.

When I became a Christian in 1982, my father, a devout Sunni Muslim, immediately disowned me. Overnight I went from having an intimate relationship with the man who was my hero to being a virtual orphan. His rejection deeply affected me. As I studied for the ministry and pastored churches, I avoided even the consideration of marriage. Until I was almost 30, I refused to imagine such a life. When I met and married Jill, my sweet, understanding wife discovered that she had married a man intractably opposed to having children. I was not obnoxious about it. I was simply resolute. No children.

You see, I was terrified of being a father.

I couldn't bear to face the possibility of hurting my children the way my father had hurt me. Even as a pastor, I did not understand intimacy. Then my first son was born. When he began speaking at about one year of age, I heard that word *Papa*. My world has not been the same since.

Describe one of your fondest memories of your father or of a father figure.

_____

God's love for us as Father far exceeds any earthly comparisons. He is not just our Father but also *Abba* Father. The term *Father* is the Greek word *Pater*, but the addition of the Aramaic term *Abba* brings a deeper dimension to our relationship with Him. The word *Abba* is an intimate term designating a child's love for his parent. In my Turkish culture the equivalent is *Baba*, or Papa.

God does not act in our lives because He is beholden to abstract principles or laws. God acts in our lives because He is our Father. No other religion speaks of such intimacy. There is no such thing as a Muslim being indwelled by God as a temple. A Hindu does not come before one of his millions of gods in intimacy.

That is one reason Christianity is not a religion. The truth that God is our Father makes Christianity a personal relationship.

The Personal God

Many faiths view God as impersonal and unknowable, so the idea of God as Father is foreign to them. When you share with Muslims, Hindus, and Buddhists, emphasize the intimacy and personal relationship that can be experienced with the God of Christianity. Be prepared to share what the Bible teaches about God's nature, but also explain the nature of your personal relationship with God by identifying ways you experience His presence and love.

This week go to someone with whom you have wanted to share Christ and ask for help with an assignment. Ask to interview him for a class in which you are studying the distinctives of Christianity, with the first one being God as Father. Interview the person and record his thoughts about God as Father.

Day 2: Christ Is Savior

The second clear line of separation between Christianity and other belief systems is that while every other system offers teachers and guides, Christ is Savior. As Paul recounted the vision he experienced at his salvation, he stated that the One who spoke to him was Jesus (see Acts 26:15). The message Christ gave to Paul is also clearly different from the message of any other belief system: the God who created also redeems.

" 'I now send you, to open their eyes that they may turn from darkness to light and from the power of Satan to God, that they may receive forgiveness of sins and a share among those who are sanctified by faith in Me.' "
Acts 26:17-18

Read in the margin Christ's words to Paul. Fill in the blanks to record the three components of Christ's message to Paul.
1. The world can turn from _____ to _____ and from the _____ of Satan to God.
2. The world can receive _____ of sins.
3. The world can be _____ by faith in Christ.

Paul was not called to present a new belief system. Paul was called to share Christ. Every other belief system offers teachings and concepts that can be separated from its founder. Remove Buddha from Buddhism, and you still have the four Noble Truths that guide a person from suffering to nirvana. Remove Muhammed from Islam, and Islam still teaches that followers have every word Allah gave in the Qur'an. In contrast, remove Jesus Christ from Christianity, and the entire system of faith collapses.

How would you explain the previous sentence to a new Christian?

_____

At the center of the Christian belief system is Christ Himself. Some mainline churches have attempted to maintain a cohesive belief system while abandoning a belief in the historical Jesus. They may try to maintain unity under a golden rule or overemphasize a search for social justice while minimizing their allegiance to the God-Man who literally came to the earth, physically died and shed His blood, and conquered death by His bodily resurrection.

Is it possible to separate Christ from Christianity? Not according to the Bible. Flowing like a current throughout the Scriptures is the central fact that our salvation and eternity are tied to Christ's nature and being.

If Jesus is not who He said He is and did not do what He said He did, then we have no hope and no salvation. Consider the following scriptural evidence.

Jesus Does Not Give Peace; He Is Our Peace

- "He is our peace, who made both groups one and tore down the dividing wall of hostility" (Eph. 2:14).
- "Now may the God of peace Himself sanctify you completely. And may your spirit, soul, and body be kept sound and blameless for the coming of our Lord Jesus Christ" (1 Thess. 5:23).
- "Since we have been declared righteous by faith, we have peace with God through our Lord Jesus Christ" (Rom. 5:1).

Jesus Does Not Provide Hope; He Is Our Hope

- "If we have placed our hope in Christ for this life only, we should be pitied more than anyone" (1 Cor. 15:19).
- "God wanted to make known to those among the Gentiles the glorious wealth of this mystery, which is Christ in you, the hope of glory" (Col. 1:27).

Jesus Does Not Give Love; He Is Love

- "The grace of our Lord overflowed, along with the faith and love that are in Christ Jesus" (1 Tim. 1:14).

CULTURE CLASH

Exclusivity: An Open Debate?

To Jesus' claim of being the one and only way to God, many in our society would echo the sentiments of this newswriter, Antonio Walker: "Christianity … has to recognize that 70 percent of humanity professes or is influenced by other religions, and that this percentage is likely to increase. … Christian churches should make every effort to show generosity to other religions by ensuring whenever possible—and it is almost always possible—that no emphasis is placed on questions that separate religions." Walker is exhorting Christians to set aside the exclusive and unique nature of Jesus and His salvation.[1]

- "Hold on to the pattern of sound teaching that you have heard from me, in the faith and love that are in Christ Jesus" (2 Tim. 1:13).

Jesus Does Not Provide Salvation and Life; He Is Salvation and Life
- "This is why I endure all things for the elect: so that they also may obtain salvation, which is in Christ Jesus, with eternal glory" (2 Tim. 2:10).
- "From childhood you have known the sacred Scriptures, which are able to instruct you for salvation through faith in Christ Jesus" (2 Tim. 3:15).

If these verses do not cause you to praise God, then perhaps this verse will: "He made the One who did not know sin to be sin for us, so that we might become the righteousness of God in Him" (2 Cor. 5:21). In other words, those previous statements emanate from the core nature of our Lord in redemption:

> *Jesus literally became sin for us so that we can*
> *become the righteousness of God through Him!*

No other belief system simultaneously presents God as both Judge and Advocate. All other systems provide a path, a guide, or a journey. In Christianity Jesus is that Path. That is the essential difference between Christianity and other faiths. It is also the reason Jesus so plainly stated:

"I am the way, the truth, and the life. No one comes to the Father except through Me" (John 14:6).

After reading the above Scriptures, what would you add to your explanation to a new Christian that Jesus is essential to Christianity?

_____

_____

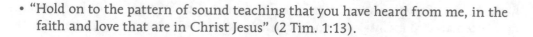

WITNESSING TIP

Share Jesus' Uniqueness

Christianity is unique among the world's religions because Jesus is unique. As the one and only Son of God who died for our sin and rose from the dead in power and victory, Jesus is the center of human history and the perfect revelation of God (see Col. 1:15-17). Only Jesus is qualified to save and to be our hope for heaven (see Rom. 5:1-2). When you witness, be ready to share the unique, biblical message of Jesus and what He means to you.

Day 3: Grace Brings Redemption

The third clear line of separation between Christianity and the world's religions is God's provision of salvation. Although Hinduism, Buddhism, and Islam discuss human sin, none of them offers a remedy that involves grace. The vital difference between Christianity and all other belief systems is grace.

Return to Paul's account of his salvation in Acts 26. As Jesus spoke to him, God's message of grace was clearly in view:

> " ¹⁷I will rescue you from the people and from the Gentiles, to whom I now send you, ¹⁸to open their eyes that they may turn from darkness to light and from the power of Satan to God, that they may receive forgiveness of sins and a share among those who are sanctified by faith in Me.' ¹⁹Therefore, King Agrippa, I was not disobedient to the heavenly vision. ²⁰Instead, I preached to those in Damascus first, and to those in Jerusalem and in all the region of Judea, and to the Gentiles, that they should repent and turn to God, and do works worthy of repentance. ²¹For this reason the Jews seized me in the temple complex and were trying to kill me. ²²Since I have obtained help that comes from God, to this day I stand and testify to both small and great, saying nothing else than what the prophets and Moses said would take place—²³that the Messiah must suffer, and that as the first to rise from the dead, He would proclaim light to our people and to the Gentiles."
> Acts 26:17-23

Reread Acts 26:17-23 and identify Christ's work on our behalf.

Verse 17: _____

Verse 18 (two actions): _____

_____

Verse 23 (two actions): _____

In numerous places in this passage, Christ detailed His work on our behalf:
- I will rescue you (v. 17).
- They may receive forgiveness of sins (v. 18).
- They may be sanctified through faith in Me (v. 18).
- The Messiah must suffer (v. 23).
- The Messiah must rise from the dead as the first One (v. 23).

This work that Christ does for us is known as grace. As the guiding principle of God's work of redemption to humanity, grace is the stark distinction of Christianity.

Few biblical texts present grace in salvation in such a clear light as Ephesians 2:4-10, in the margin. Underline each thing grace accomplishes for us.

"God, who is abundant in mercy, because of His great love that He had for us, made us alive with the Messiah even though we were dead in trespasses. By grace you are saved! He also raised us up with Him and seated us with Him in the heavens, in Christ Jesus, so that in the coming ages He might display the immeasurable riches of His grace in His kindness to us in Christ Jesus. ... For by grace you are saved through faith, and this is not from yourselves; it is God's gift—not from works, so that no one can boast. For we are His creation—created in Christ Jesus for good works, which God prepared ahead of time so that we should walk in them."
Ephesians 2:4-10

In clarion terminology Paul defined *grace* as Christ's offer of salvation. Christ provides salvation for us because we could not provide it for ourselves. Grace is also inextricably tied to mercy. An old Christian proverb states:

> *Mercy is not receiving what I deserve.*
> *Grace is receiving what I do not deserve.*

The concept of grace is absent from every major world religion. In every other belief system each individual is left to his own obedience and his own works to earn salvation. In Hinduism the caste into which you will be reincarnated entirely depends on your journey on earth. In Buddhism your response to suffering and the Eightfold Path determines your destiny. In Islam each person is born with balanced scales; every work in life will be weighed in the balance.

Only in Christianity do our inherent sinfulness and inability to live by the law result in God's provision of grace. God, knowing humans' incapacity for righteousness, does for us what we cannot do for ourselves. Furthermore, grace not only saves us but also permeates our very existence. Children of God are guided by, infused with, and sustained by His grace.

Rank the following nine provisions of grace from the most important to you to the least important by writing the appropriate number beside each passage.

Christ Died Because of Grace
"We do see Jesus—made lower than the angels for a short time so that by God's grace He might taste death for everyone—crowned with glory and honor because of the suffering of death" (Heb. 2:9). ____

Grace Justifies Us
"Having been justified by His grace, we may become heirs with the hope of eternal life" (Titus 3:7). ____

Grace Strengthens Us
"You, therefore, my child, be strong in the grace that is in Christ Jesus" (2 Tim. 2:1). ____

Grace Gives Us Purpose
"[God] has saved us and called us with a holy calling, not according to our works, but according to His own purpose and grace, which was given to us in Christ Jesus before time began. This has now been made evident through the appearing of our Savior Christ Jesus, who has abolished death and has brought life and immortality to light through the gospel" (2 Tim. 1:9-10). ____

Grace Encourages Us
"May our Lord Jesus Christ Himself and God our Father, who has loved us and given us eternal encouragement and good hope by grace" (2 Thess. 2:16). ____

Grace Unites Us
"It is right for me to think this way about all of you, because I have you in my heart, and you are all partners with me in grace, both in my imprisonment and in the defense and establishment of the gospel" (Phil. 1:7). ____

Grace Allows Us to Use Our Gifts
"Grace was given to each one of us according to the measure of the Messiah's gift" (Eph. 4:7). ____

Grace Sustains Us in Trouble
"He said to me, 'My grace is sufficient for you, for power is perfected in weakness.' Therefore, I will most gladly boast all the more about my weaknesses, so that Christ's power may reside in me" (2 Cor. 12:9). ____

Grace Sanctifies Us
"God is able to make every grace overflow to you, so that in every way, always having everything you need, you may excel in every good work" (2 Cor. 9:8). ____

Did you have difficulty assigning a rank to the many functions of grace in our lives? I certainly do. Some religious people have offered the indictment that grace is Christians' excuse to sin as we desire since we will be forgiven regardless. Muslims often intone that grace is Christians' invention to assuage the guilt of sinful lives. Yet the Bible anticipates this argument, as Jesus' half-brother Jude aptly stated: "Certain men, who were designated for this judgment long ago, have come in by stealth; they are ungodly, turning the grace of our God into promiscuity and denying our only Master and Lord, Jesus Christ" (Jude 4).

If we have truly surrendered to Christ as Master and Lord, we could never habitually descend into the anarchy and addiction of promiscuity. Doing so would reject the Lord to whom we had supposedly given our hearts. It would not only contradict salvation but also abdicate grace.

Perhaps you consider today's study somewhat pedestrian. You have studied grace throughout your Christian walk and could recite some of these verses in your sleep. Why do we go to such lengths to illustrate such a simple Christian concept?

Because grace is foreign to the rest of the world.

For many of us who came to Christianity from another world religion, grace is a profound and startling principle. We were taught that we must live and die by our works. We grew up with the constant terror of the balancing scales. We learned to face death with loathing because we knew we were unprepared for judgment.

Yet when confronted with grace, we were befuddled. Do you mean that Christ has given me the means for my salvation? Are you saying that I cannot be good enough? Do you honestly teach that where God knows I am incapable, He instead provides His blood as my means of salvation?

The answers, of course, are yes. That is precisely what the Bible teaches.

Grace reduces many of us to tears of gratitude. As a former Muslim who was taught that paradise is promised for those who die fighting in the cause of Islam, I will put it in the most graphic terms:

> *By grace Jesus Christ strapped Himself to a cross*
> *so that I would not have to strap a bomb to myself.*

Does that help illustrate grace for you? Jesus shed His blood by grace, and as a result, my blood is both insufficient and unnecessary.

I want you to remember the degrees of separation that distinguish Christianity from every other belief system. Review them as necessary and list the three we have covered so far. Only Christianity provides—

1. God as _____;
2. Christ as _____;
3. _____ that brings redemption.

WITNESSING TIP

Highlight Grace

Every belief system except Christianity teaches salvation by works; many people even mistakenly define a Christian as someone who does good works. As you cultivate witnessing relationships, try to discover the lost person's concept of salvation. Is he or she depending on good works, ancestry, ethnicity—or the blood of Christ? As a Christian, commit yourself to doing good works as an expression of your salvation that came to you by God's grace alone. Then be prepared to explain why you do good for others.

Day 4: The World Is Our Mission Field

In his speech to King Agrippa, Paul enunciated a fourth clear line of distinction between Christianity and all other belief systems: Christ offers salvation and hope to the world. In Paul's encounter with Jesus on the Damascus Road, Jesus had told him: " 'I will rescue you from the people and from the Gentiles, to whom I now send you, to open their eyes that they may turn from darkness to light and from the power of Satan to God, that they may receive forgiveness of sins and a share among those who are sanctified by faith in Me.' He would proclaim light to our people and to the Gentiles" (Acts 26:17-18,23).

These words must have struck Agrippa as strange. Was Paul actually saying that Jesus had called him to preach to everyone?

Every other system in the world operates by an us-versus-them mentality. The heathen and pagan are to be rejected. The infidel is to be converted or killed. The nonbeliever is outside the purview of the gods. Yet God calls us to a radical concept:

We are commanded to love our enemies and to share Jesus with those who hate us. Christ died for the world.

In your own words explain why the world is a Christian's mission field.

_____

_____

This idea separates Christianity from every other belief system. From the beginning of Scripture, all of humanity is drawn from the same lineage. Therefore, we are related to every person on earth, dating back to Adam and Eve. Christ commands us to view the world through His eyes of love.

Read 1 Timothy 2:1-8 in the margin and fill in the blanks to identify those Christ came to save.
Prayers should be made for _____ (see v. 1).
God wants _____ to be saved (see vv. 3-4).
God wants _____ to come to the knowledge of the truth (see v. 4).
Jesus gave Himself a ransom for _____ (see v. 6).

As Paul advised the young pastor in Ephesus, he spoke of the mission field for which he labored:
- Prayers should be made for everyone (see 1 Tim. 2:1).
- God our Savior wants everyone to be saved (see 1 Tim. 2:3-4).
- God wants everyone to come to the knowledge of the truth (see 1 Tim. 2:4).
- Christ Jesus gave Himself a ransom for all (see 1 Tim. 2:6).

It couldn't be any clearer: Jesus Christ came to save everyone—every brutal world dictator, every terrorist, even those who blaspheme His name.

It is humbling to realize the reach of Christ's love and the extent of His offer of salvation. As a visitor to my first church, I was bewildered by church members' kindness. I could not imagine why they—having never met me—kept extending such hospitality toward me. When I finally mustered the courage to ask, their response opened my eyes to the breadth of Christ's love. The exchange went something like this:

Me: "Why are you being so nice to me? You do not even know me."
Them: "We are nice to everyone."
Me: "But I am a Muslim. I am different from you."
Them: "Yes, but that is the way Jesus Christ loved us."

"¹*First of all, then, I urge that petitions, prayers, intercessions, and thanksgivings be made for everyone, ²for kings and all those who are in authority, so that we may lead a tranquil and quiet life in all godliness and dignity. ³This is good, and it pleases God our Savior, ⁴who wants everyone to be saved and to come to the knowledge of the truth. ⁵For there is one God and one mediator between God and man, a man, Christ Jesus, ⁶who gave Himself—a ransom for all, a testimony at the proper time. ⁷For this I was appointed a herald, an apostle (I am telling the truth; I am not lying), and a teacher of the Gentiles in faith and truth. ⁸Therefore I want the men in every place to pray, lifting up holy hands without anger or argument.*"
1 Timothy 2:1-8

I did not understand until someone showed me this verse: "God proves His own love for us in that while we were still sinners Christ died for us!" (Rom. 5:8).

The only true differences in this world are not along racial, geographic, financial, or political lines. Men and women are either saved or lost. If Christ died to save lost men and women (and He did), then the appropriate response of a saved person is to love the lost person the same way Christ loved us. While we were still immersed in our sin and at war with Him, Christ loved us.

Are you growing in obedience to Jesus' call to love all people? Place an X on the continuum to represent your willingness to love five years ago and a check (✓) to represent that capacity today.

Not very loving   **Sacrificially loving all people**

What evidence in your life indicates that you are growing in your willingness to love all people?

_____

_____

_____

Jesus taught during the Sermon on the Mount, " 'I tell you, love your enemies, and pray for those who persecute you' " (Matt. 5:44). In an even more telling statement, Jesus said: " 'Love your enemies, do [what is] good, and lend, expecting nothing in return. Then your reward will be great, and you will be sons of the Most High. For He is gracious to the ungrateful and evil' " (Luke 6:35).

This teaching is vitally different from that of all world religions. Although some belief systems call for universal conversion, the only other option offered is conquest. Convert them or kill them. Only Christianity calls men and women to love those who hate us.

The massive numbers of adherents to other belief systems are daunting, as the chart on page 23 indicates. While in some cases the numbers are inflated, they are equally inflated.[2] Not everyone who claims to be a Christian is actually a born-again believer. However, the growth of the four world religions we are studying is consistent. Hinduism, Buddhism, Judaism (in some areas), and Islam are growing at explosive rates.

Religion	World Population	American Population
Christianity	2 billion	160 million
Islam	1.3 billion	4–8 million
Buddhism	376 million	2–4 million
Hinduism	900 million	1–2 million
Judaism	15 million	3–4 million

Some studies estimate that these world religions will bypass major mainline Christian denominations in just a few years.

Just as the world's mission fields are ready for harvest (see John 4:35), so are our fields in America. As dramatic examples, between 1990 and 2000 in the United States, Buddhists and Hindus grew at rates of 170 and 237 percent, respectively, while Muslims increased between 100 and 150 percent. These growth trends are expected to continue.

Many of the lost men and women who adhere to these belief systems have come to our shores. Because they are people for whom Christ died, they are our mission fields.

WITNESSING TIP

Open Your Eyes

Today America is a patchwork of world religions. You are likely to encounter people from various religious backgrounds at work, in the marketplace, or in your neighborhood. These are people God has placed in your life for a reason. Instead of ignoring them, ask Him to give you eyes to see their spiritual needs and a heart to share Christ with compassion.

As you develop relationships, be willing to learn about their faith, ask questions, build on commonalities, define terms, and respond with love and acceptance. These actions may give you the opportunity to share the good news of Jesus.

" 'Open your eyes and look at the fields, for they are ready for harvest.' "
John 4:35

Day 5: Christ Gives Literal and Eternal Life

The final lines of separation between Christianity and other belief systems deal with eternity. The fact that Christ gives eternal life is the fifth degree of separation. Only Christianity offers a God who is beyond time. Both Hinduism and Buddhism view time as cyclical; that is, time is a vast circle, repeating itself. In Christianity time has a beginning, a middle, and an end. Christ is forever the light of heaven; therefore, we will have no need for watches in eternity. We will live forever with Him.

The Way to Heaven

According to The Barna Group, nearly two-thirds of Americans expect to find themselves in heaven after their deaths. While many indicated their belief was based on an acceptance of Jesus Christ, many others indicated that they had earned that destination by obedience to the Ten Commandments (15 percent), being a good person (15 percent), or similar works. Even among born-again Christians, half of those surveyed indicated a belief that someone could earn salvation through good works.[3]

"He is also the head of the body, the church; He is the beginning, the firstborn from the dead, so that He might come to have first place in everything."
Colossians 1:18

"... from Jesus Christ, the faithful witness, the first-born from the dead and the ruler of the kings of the earth. To Him who loves us and has set us free from our sins by His blood."
Revelation 1:5

The sixth degree of separation is Christ's physical and literal conquest of death. Jesus literally died, and He literally rose from the dead. His resurrection is key to the Christian faith.

Read the verses in the margin and underline the phrase that is common to both verses.

Did you notice each verse's reference to Christ as the first to conquer death and the grave? Hebrews 12:23 also refers to the church as the "assembly of the firstborn." The implication is clear: Jesus' conquest of death has eternal consequences for you and me.

In Revelation Jesus stated, " 'I was dead, but look—I am alive forever and ever, and I hold the keys of death and Hades' " (Rev. 1:18). In eternity we physically follow Him in His conquest of death because He was the first to rise from the dead.

Christ's resurrection was a stumbling point for those who charged Paul before Agrippa. As Paul asked, " 'Why is it considered incredible by any of you that God raises the dead?' " (Acts 26:8). Paul spoke of having an actual—not mystical or imagined—conversation with Jesus. The Lord was really alive. Paul argued that the resurrection was the impetus for his work (see Acts 26:23).

If Jesus Christ did not actually die and then literally rise, then Paul did not actually speak with Him, and God did not actually call him to preach. Christ's proclamation pivots on the fact that He conquered death. The entire gospel message of salvation is validated by Christ's resurrection to life. Paul made this point in his first letter to the Corinthian Christians:

> If Christ is preached as raised from the dead, how can some of you say, "There is no resurrection of the dead"? But if there is no resurrection of the dead, then Christ has not been raised; and if Christ has not been raised, then our preaching is without foundation, and so is your faith. In addition, we are found to be false witnesses about God, because we have testified about God that He raised up Christ—whom He did not raise up if in fact the dead are not raised. For if the dead are not raised, Christ has not been raised. And if Christ has not been raised, your faith is worthless; you are still in your sins. Therefore those who have fallen asleep in Christ have also perished. If we have placed our hope in Christ for this life only, we should be pitied more than anyone. 1 Corinthians 15:12-19

Explain in your own words why Christ's resurrection is pivotal to the Christian faith.

_____

_____

Christ's resurrection is at the center of the Christian faith. If Jesus did not rise from the dead, then all of Christianity is false.

Fill in the blanks to identify the six degrees of separation that distinguish Christianity from other belief systems.

1. God is _____.

2. Christ is _____.

3. _____ brings redemption.

4. The _____ is our mission field.

5. Christ gives _____ life.

6. Christ literally conquered _____.

Now explain in your own words why Christianity is not a religion.

_____

_____

_____

_____

_____

Christianity cannot be a religion. In religion humanity reaches toward God. Christianity inverts the process: as a loving Father, God reaches for humanity. Grace, rather than works, is offered as the means of salvation for all people. Salvation is a work of God, not of humans. Christianity is not a system but a Savior. And because of His triumph over death by His resurrection, we will also be resurrected and will spend eternity with Him.

WITNESSING TIP

Proclaim That He Is Alive

Christians' confidence in life after death is not based on wish fulfillment or stories of near-death experiences. We base our hope for eternal life on the historical event of Christ's resurrection. Here are some evidences of Christ's resurrection you can share with an unbeliever: the empty tomb (see John 20:1-18), eyewitness reports of Jesus' physical appearances (see Acts 1:3; 1 Cor. 15:3-8), the founding of the church (see Acts 2:41), and the apostles' fearless preaching of the gospel at the cost of their lives (see Acts 4:1-22; 5:17-42; 7:54-60).

Believers are separate from world religions but not from religious people. To use the language of the Reformation, we are called to be profane Christians. The phrase *profane Christians* does not speak of our language or demeanor. In the classic Latin sense, *profane* means *outside the temple*. We are called to go outside our temples into a religious world to share the gospel of the One who died for all.

This week we were on familiar ground. We are about to enter much less familiar territory. But I hope you will realize the critical need to learn to explain the distinctives of your faith.

---

[1] Ted Olsen, compiler, "Weblog: Think Jesus Is the Only Way to Heaven? You're a Terrorist Waiting to Happen," *Christianity Today* [online], 29 October 2001 [cited 5 May 2005]. Available from the Internet: *www.christianitytoday.com*.

[2] "Major Religions of the World Ranked by Number of Adherents" and "Largest Religious Groups in the United States of America" [cited 10 May 2005]. Available from the Internet: *www.adherents.com*. The differences between the numbers depend on an accurate identification of the religions' true followers. For instance, some surveys include Mormonism and Roman Catholicism in the Christian category. For simplicity's sake, we have left the Christian number ambiguous, although we are certain that the actual number of born-again believers is far fewer than the chart indicates. The American Religious Data Archive (ARDA) and the American Religious Identity Survey (ARIS) also include heritage as a deciding factor. For example, many who claim to be Jewish may actually be atheists, but they are Jewish in heritage. The only equalizer is that all major religions struggle with the issue of defining legitimate followers.

[3] "Americans Describe Their Views About Life After Death," *The Barna Update* [online], 21 October 2003 [cited 10 May 2005]. Available from the Internet: *www.barna.org*.

Viewer Guide
Group Session 1

Review Segment: Six Degrees of Separation

The central core of the Scriptures is that Jesus Christ came to _____ religion.

The things that distinguish us also change the way we approach the _____.
- We live in a personal, intimate _____ with the God who created us.
- We operate in _____ _____.
- In Christianity we don't have a teacher; we have a _____.
- We live by _____, and works are out of _____.

We are separate from the religious world because they seek ways to _____ their gods.

In Christianity it isn't that man seeks _____. God seeks _____.

The cross put an end to our vain, prideful, desperate search for _____.

Teaching Segment: Politically Correct, Biblically Corrupt

The Parthenon represents the worldview of _____ civilization.
Here every god is _____.

Everybody's _____ about something. Everybody has a _____.

Everyone wants to be free from _____.
Everyone wants to be free from _____.
Everybody wants a _____.
Everybody wants a _____.

Every church and every Christian is defined by how they approach culture:
- Christ _____ culture
- Christ _____ or oblivious to culture
- Christ _____ culture

Christianity _____ culture means we find ways to bridge into their lives.
We not only know how to present the gospel, we also know the _____ they will ask and the _____ in which they live.

Superstition and spiritualism have replaced absolute _____ and biblical

_____ in many places.

Politically Correct, Biblically Corrupt

Worldview Overview and the

Theology of the Coffeehouse

While Paul was waiting for them in Athens, his spirit was troubled within him when he saw that the city was full of idols. So he reasoned in the synagogue with the Jews and with those who worshiped God, and in the marketplace every day with those who happened to be there. Then also, some of the Epicurean and Stoic philosophers argued with him. Some said, "What is the pseudo-intellectual trying to say?"

Others replied, "He seems to be a preacher of foreign deities"—because he was telling the good news about Jesus and the resurrection.

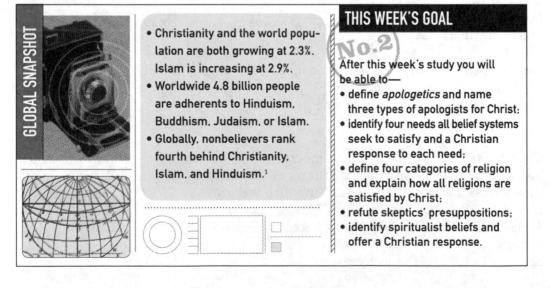

GLOBAL SNAPSHOT

- Christianity and the world population are both growing at 2.3%. Islam is increasing at 2.9%.
- Worldwide 4.8 billion people are adherents to Hinduism, Buddhism, Judaism, or Islam.
- Globally, nonbelievers rank fourth behind Christianity, Islam, and Hinduism.[1]

THIS WEEK'S GOAL

No.2

After this week's study you will be able to—

- define *apologetics* and name three types of apologists for Christ;
- identify four needs all belief systems seek to satisfy and a Christian response to each need;
- define four categories of religion and explain how all religions are satisfied by Christ;
- refute skeptics' presuppositions;
- identify spiritualist beliefs and offer a Christian response.

They took him and brought him to the Areopagus, and said, "May we learn about this new teaching you're speaking of? For what you say sounds strange to us, and we want to know what these ideas mean." Now all the Athenians and the foreigners residing there spent their time on nothing else but telling or hearing something new. Acts 17:16-21

The Theater of the Opinionated

To say our culture is in chaos is an understatement. Everywhere we look—on television, in schools, in the news media—the world seems to be rushing headlong into the abyss without the slightest consideration for the consequences. Yet specifying how our culture operates is more difficult. As I have spent hundreds of hours on campuses across the nation and in media interviews, I have speculated on the overarching themes that drive our culture at large. It is the world in which we live, and it isn't pretty.

- ***A culture of victimization:*** no one is responsible.
- ***A culture of syncretism:*** all religions are the same.
- ***A culture of relativism:*** all religions are equally true.
- ***A culture of confrontation***: how loudly people state their opinions is more important than the content of their messages.
- ***A culture of hyphenation:*** people are invested in movements and causes, based on their subgroup or movement, and they define themselves by this hyphenation.
- ***A culture of medication:*** we treat the symptoms but not the core diseases of yearning, guilt, and pain.

Welcome to the modern-day theater of the opinionated.

How does a Christian respond in such a cacophony of voices? In 1951 H. Richard Niebuhr wrote *Christ and Culture*, in which he outlined the positions Christians typically take in regard to culture. We have modified his results, but think about where you or your church would fit:

- ***Christ above culture:*** Christians are oblivious to the culture around them.
- ***Christ against culture:*** Christians take an adversarial stance against anything culture offers.
- ***Christ of culture:*** Christians attempt to mimic anything popular in culture.[2]

How do you think the Apostle Paul would approach culture? Look again at the text on page 28. Paul was in the marketplace, presenting Christ to the philosophers and the common people. He was squarely in the middle of his world, without fear or flinching. I would suggest that Paul offers a fourth alternative for responding to our culture:

- ***Christ confronting culture:*** Christians neither hide from evil nor assimilate it. Surrounded by sin, Christians confront it and persuade the sinful to come to Christ. This is a believer's stance. We are not oblivious to culture, nor do we shrink from it. We are not silenced by culture. Instead, we present Christ with every available tool and in every possible context.

As you study this week, keep in mind the opportunities God gives you to present Christ—at the grocery store, at the gym, and in your workplace. Paul has shown us it is possible to provoke our world with Christ while maintaining a holy stance.

Day 1: Three Types of Christians Who Confront Culture

It is one thing to say that we want to present Christ in every context. It is quite another to establish a method for following through. How does the average Christian find a way to present Jesus as the One who can meet every need?

In generations past, churches trained their members to go door-to-door and, when the occupant opened it, to deliver a gospel presentation. This method has drawbacks in our present day. Now most people, skeptical and cynical, slam the door before we get past the first paragraph. In addition, few encounters with our friends ever lend themselves to a perfect opening to present the gospel.

Therefore, I would like to submit another option: engage unbelievers in a discussion of their beliefs as a way to introduce Christ. Certainly that was Paul's approach in Acts 17:17: "He reasoned in the synagogue with the Jews and with those who worshiped God, and in the marketplace every day with those who happened to be there."

I can already hear the objections to this method: "I don't like fights." "I get uncomfortable in confrontation." "I don't think quickly on my feet." Never fear. The Bible offers three alternatives to presenting Christ. These methods all fit under the broad umbrella of apologetics, which means *a logical and reasoned defense of your faith in the context of objection.* Your goal in apologetics is to reach a point that you can present Jesus Christ.

The Bible offers hope to everyone who wants to be an apologist for Christ, regardless of your personality. Consider the following three biblical options.

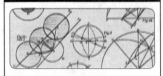

Positive Apologetics: You Are Barnabas

You hate fighting. When tempers rise, you leave the room. You are most comfortable engaging in positive apologetics. A positive apologist is someone who does not want to challenge someone else's beliefs. However, you sincerely want to share your faith in Jesus Christ. Like Paul, you want "to know nothing among you except Jesus Christ and Him crucified" (1 Cor. 2:1-4). Although you disdain fighting and arguing, you do not want to hide your witness. Instead, you want to find ways to bring your faith in Him into the discussion.

A positive apologist offers his or her testimony to those who are hurting. You exude sympathy, and people in crisis are drawn to you. You are soft-spoken and kind, and your heart for others is a winsome tool for God to use.

Immediately, Billy Graham comes to mind, doesn't he? Have you noticed that whatever the issue or event, Dr. Graham finds a way to draw the discussion to Christ and salvation? All of his books, all of his sermons, and all of his political involvement seem to transcend culture and speak to everyone.

Let's look at a New Testament character who was a positive apologist.

Read Acts 4:35-37 in the margin and write the meaning of the name Barnabas. _____

Barnabas was an important worker in the early church. The Scripture you read demonstrates why he was aptly named Son of Encouragement. In more than 20 references to Barnabas in the New Testament, he is seen as a peacemaker and an encourager. For example, he attempted to mitigate the disagreement between Paul and Mark (see Acts 15:39). In Acts 15:25 Luke called Barnabas *beloved*. However, this quality does not diminish Barnabas's boldness (see Acts 13:46).

WITNESSING TIP

Build Bridges

Through your words and actions, build bridges of understanding and witness with unbelievers. Relationships can be established through listening, acts of kindness, encouragement, recreation, and sacrificial service. Perhaps the person has needs that can be met through more formal ministries such as literacy or crisis pregnancy. Communicate unconditional love, but always move toward a time when you present the good news of Jesus Christ. In addition, never compromise your faith in order to preserve a friendship.

"This was then distributed to each person as anyone had a need. Joseph, a Levite and Cypriot by birth, whom the apostles named Barnabas, which is translated Son of Encouragement, sold a field he owned, brought the money, and laid it as the apostles' feet."
Acts 4:35-37

Read Acts 15:2 in the margin. How did Barnabas respond to a controversy?

_____

"After Paul and Barnabas had engaged them in serious argument and debate, they arranged for Paul and Barnabas and some others of them to go up to the apostles and elders in Jerusalem concerning this controversy."
Acts 15:2

Barnabas engaged in "serious argument and debate" with the Jerusalem leaders over the church's mission. This incident shows that Barnabas's encouraging character did not prevent his boldness in speaking the truth.

Barnabas was both bold and relational. Those are excellent qualities for a Christian apologist today. We should be careful, however, to let the Holy Spirit govern our expression of these qualities. Our challenge is to be bold without being confrontational. We are also challenged to develop relationships for the purpose of sharing Christ. If we cultivate relationships but never get around to sharing, we haven't fulfilled our mission as an apologist for Christ.

How do you react to this approach of positive apologetics?
○ **It gives me hope; I can do that.**
○ **It's too wimpy for me. Let's get down to brass tacks.**
○ **I'm afraid I won't know what to say.**

What danger lies in taking the positive approach? _____

_____

31

Negative Apologetics: You Are Paul

You relish a good debate. You pride yourself in never backing down. The prospect of getting into a heated exchange revs you up. You actually find yourself finishing arguments … in your car … alone … yelling at no one in particular. This is not to say that you are mean or ill-tempered. You are simply clear in your beliefs, and everyone knows it. You refer to yourself as opinionated. Others may characterize you as obnoxious.

Sound familiar? You are a modern Apostle Paul, and you are not alone. Many of us share in your predilection. I know I do. Like the Apostle Paul, everywhere you go, arguments potentially follow. You can dissect the fallacies in other belief systems in a moment, and you are unafraid to share your Christian beliefs.

This approach to discussing faith is called negative apologetics. Philosophers call it polemics. A polemicist (also called negative apologist) is someone who defends Christianity by illuminating the deficiencies of other systems. In Athens Paul referred to the pantheon of false gods and then proclaimed Christ to the exclusion of the others. A negative apologist often says: "It is not enough just to present the positive case for Christ. Before people can get saved, they must first realize they are lost. Repentance demands that we abandon all other gods as idols and all other systems as wrong."

Do you see yourself as a negative apologist? ○ **Yes**   ○ **No**

Check what you think might be the primary danger in this approach.
○ **Resorting to physical violence**
○ **Developing a hateful heart**
○ **Failing to introduce the truth of Jesus Christ**

A major warning for a polemicist is the danger of developing a hateful heart. A polemicist must keep in mind:

> *This is not about winning arguments.*
> *This is about winning souls.*

A polemicist would do well to remember James's admonition: "Everyone must be quick to hear, slow to speak, and slow to anger" (Jas. 1:19).

Contextual Apologetics: You Are Peter

A contextual apologist is someone who uses a current cultural issue, crisis, or event to draw the discussion to Christ. Our Lord Jesus did this often, as seen in John 4, where He used the well to refer to Himself as the Living Water. His parables masterfully used situations and language to illustrate a profound point.

In the apostolic church Peter often used arguments in the streets to make his point. On the day of Pentecost some people murmured that the Christians must have been drunk. Peter, hearing their charges, quickly rose and said: " 'Jewish men and all you

"Jesus said, 'Everyone who drinks from this water will get thirsty again. But whoever drinks from the water that I will give him will never get thirsty again—ever! In fact, the water I will give him will become a well of water springing up within him for eternal life.' "
John 4:13-14

residents of Jerusalem, let this be known to you and pay attention to my words. For these people are not drunk, as you suppose, since it's only nine in the morning' " (Acts 2:14-15). For a cultural apologist it's not about confrontation. It's about illustration.

Contextual apologists often use a popular song or movie title to make a point about the Christian experience. Although they do not necessarily affirm the message conveyed by thc items or events, they use these things to launch a discussion about faith.

The inherent difficulty in this method is that we can become so enamored with the world's culture that we become sympathetic to it. It is one thing to use culture's music, art, literature, and entertainment. It is quite another to let those entities use you.

Complete the definition of apologetics: A logical and reasoned _____ of your faith in the context of _____.

Review by matching the type of apologetics with the correct biblical example.
___ 1. Contextual   **a. Barnabas**
___ 2. Positive   **b. Paul**
___ 3. Negative   **c. Peter**

Check the approach that is most comfortable for you in discussing your faith and in presenting the gospel.
○ **Positive apologetics**   ○ **Negative apologetics**   ○ **Cultural apologetics**

Why do you think this approach suits you? _____

Day 2: Four Needs All Belief Systems Seek to Satisfy

When Paul was speaking with the religious leaders and philosophers in Athens, his message was singled out as unique: "Some of the Epicurean and Stoic philosophers argued with him. Some said, 'What is this pseudo-intellectual trying to say?' Others replied, 'He seems to be a preacher of foreign deities'—because he was telling the good news about Jesus and the resurrection" (Acts 17:18). This reaction is especially astonishing given the fact that hundreds of philosophers gathered in public every day.

Paul was offering forgiveness and eternal life. Paul was proclaiming Christ as the One who conquered death. Paul was standing in the midst of the philosophers and contradicting every single system at the same time, and his listeners objected.

Luke singled out two distinct groups who illustrated the variety of philosophies that battled for people's minds. The Epicureans believed that by indulging in the flesh, people could find salvation and meaning. The Stoics found meaning in denying the flesh and emotions. Into this mix Paul stood and proclaimed Christ. On the one hand, Christ died an ignominious and cruel death, so He would offend the Epicureans. On the other hand, Paul was preaching the good news of the resurrection, so his preaching of joy, hope, and meaning would appall the Stoics.

Strangely, those objections continue to this day. The God-Man, Jesus Christ, flies in the face of every major world religion. While some construct a strange mythology of two gods fighting over humankind and others seek to find meaning and purpose in ethics, only Christianity finds solace in the person of Christ.

We can make an interesting observation about the reaction to Paul's message:

Though they all violently disagreed with Paul's answers,
they still sought answers to the same questions.

Humankind, beset with sin, evil, and suffering, still asks the same universal questions. Therefore, each belief system must satisfy the human longing for coherence and purpose. No matter what system is discussed—Native American, Oriental, Occidental, Middle Eastern, or Far Eastern—every world religion strives to address the following four universal cravings.

The Desire for Knowledge

Every world religion seeks to inform. From birth, humans are inquisitive about the profound questions of existence. You don't have to teach, train, or prod a child to ask these questions. They simply do.

When my son Braxton turned five years old, he became a virtual why machine. Why is the sun yellow? Why does the moon glow? Every night as I read him a story and prayed with him, he would pepper me with questions:

- Where does God live?
- How does God hear us?
- Does God know everything?
- Why did Jesus die?
- Does the Devil live in my closet?
- Why are you bald when other fathers have hair?

These are not simply the impulses of an inquisitive child; they are part of the larger questions of life. Where do I fit in? Where am I going? Why do I hurt? Each belief system seeks to answer those questions.

The answers of the world's belief systems fit into three categories:

1. Theism: God or gods have communicated the answers.
2. Buddhism: enlightened men or women have discovered the answers.
3. Deism: you should not seek answers but peace.

In other words, you should (1) listen to God or the gods, (2) listen to our leader, or (3) stop asking.

Theistic religions, like Judaism and Islam, believe that human beings have a purpose and that God has communicated this purpose to us. Christianity agrees with this view.

Read 2 Timothy 3:16 in the margin. Name one way God communicates to us.

_____

Read Hebrews 1:1-2 in the margin. What are two other ways God has communicated to us?

_____

_____

In the past God revealed His purpose and His ways through the prophets. Today we look to God's Word and to God's supreme revelation in His Son to discover God's purpose for our lives.

Systems such as Buddhism do not necessarily rely on a god per se but rather offer answers from leaders whom they deem enlightened or wise. Deistic systems do not deny a god or gods, but they see a creator as irrelevant. The journey to find the answers, regardless of where it takes you, is more important than the answers. This final category illustrates modern secular systems such as relativism and existentialism.

My son was never satisfied with the "Because I said so" answer, and neither are most men and women. They want to know the why. This is especially important since humankind has now developed the capacity to do many things, such as genetic cloning, without answering the question of *whether* we should do them.

The Desire for Community

Every belief system seeks to make its followers feel that they are part of a great cause or purpose. Helping followers feel accepted into the fold is essential to building community. Even belief systems that do not teach grace, such as Islam, have an elaborate brotherhood that seeks to unite followers; it also serves to shape them into a force. Similarly, Buddhism unites followers in a common journey toward nirvana.

As any Christian can attest, fellowship is vital in building unity in the body of Christ. One proof lies in the fact that most Christians who leave their church do not do so because of false doctrine but because of a break in the fellowship. All churches, great and small, consist of smaller fellowships such as Sunday School classes, cell groups, discipleship groups, or support groups. These communities create unity around a common purpose and cultivate a sense of belonging.

Modern-day Christian community is modeled on the early church in the Book of Acts. Although the persecution was intense, the early believers were drawn together in the common bond of fellowship.

"All Scripture is inspired by God and is profitable for teaching, for rebuking, for correcting, for training in righteousness."
2 Timothy 3:16

"Long ago God spoke to the fathers by the prophets at different times and in different ways. In these last days, [God] has spoken to us by His Son, whom He has appointed heir of all things and through who He made the universe."
Hebrews 1:1-2

DEFINITION

Relativism

A belief that all religions are equally true. To say that your religion or system is right is the highest sin to a relativist. To a relativist, everyone is right, or at the very least, everyone has the right to be right.

Existentialism

A system of belief that depends entirely on emotion and feeling. There is no normative or absolute standard. Instead, individuals find their specific answers, which become truth to them.

Read the verses in the margin and underline components of the early believers' fellowship.

According to these verses, the early believers enjoyed fellowship through prayer, one another's company, teaching, meals, and mutual sharing. The desire for fellowship in Christianity has spiritual significance because when we come together, we do so in Christ's name and in His love. Christ Himself is the source of our sense of community.

"All these were continually united in prayer."
Acts 1:14

"When the day of Pentecost had arrived, they were all together in one place."
Acts 2:1

"They devoted themselves to the apostles' teaching, to fellowship, to the breaking of bread, and to prayers."
Acts 2:42

"All the believers were together and had everything in common."
Acts 2:44

The Desire for Freedom from Guilt

Every belief system attempts to deal with humanity's innate knowledge of sin. The Bible tells us that this awareness of sin is caused by our common guilt in Adam (see Rom. 5:12-21), but all systems acknowledge the need for people to rid themselves of evil. Even belief systems that teach that all evil and sin are illusions, such as Hinduism, admit that people feel guilty because of that illusion.

Every people group in history has attempted to deal with some concept of wrong, sin, guilt, or evil. Even so-called advanced Western civilizations that are humanistic (atheistic) attempt to deal with guilt. If you do not believe this premise, then why do people go to therapists? Even the science of psychotherapy attempts to help people reconcile their feelings of inadequacy, pain, and guilt—or their denial of these realities. Doctors medicate those who find no answers and commit those who give in to their impulses. Yet they deal with the consequences of guilt nonetheless.

How does humanism define guilt? Some see guilt as a remnant of the evolutionary process. We feel guilty because we have evolved to the point that we can do more than we were once able to do. Others see guilt as a sign of weakness. When we succeed in an endeavor and step over others to accomplish our goal, we feel sheepish and bad about our behavior. Yet those who believe that success is good enough see guilt as a vestige of our lower state. They respond: "We won. Stop feeling guilty. The people we beat deserved their destiny."

Most religions, however, define guilt in direct correlation to their actions before their gods. When primitive islanders throw a woman into a volcano to assuage their guilt, they believe her death will make them feel better. Because the virgin atoned for their bad actions, they no longer feel sorry nor guilty. Other systems, such as modern Judaism, see life as a balanced scale. If you do more good than bad, the benevolence of the good outweighs the guilt of the bad.

Only in Christianity is a person judged by a righteous God. Humans are both conspicuously evil because of what they do and inherently evil because they are born that way.

If you catch a child with his hand in the proverbial cookie jar, what does he usually do?
○ **Confess** ○ **Run** ○ **Lie** ○ **Create a diversion**

Nine times out of 10, the child lies to avoid punishment. You don't have to train a child to do this. It is innate. The reason is that people are born sinful.

After counting the troops against God's specific injunction, "David's conscience troubled him. ... He said to the LORD, 'I have sinned greatly in what I've done. Now, LORD, because I've been very foolish, please take away Your servant's guilt' " (2 Sam. 24:10). Here David was ascribing his guilt to his actions. Most belief systems would concur. Yet when Ezra examined human nature, he saw something far more insidious—humankind's desire for sin. This sin obsession goes far deeper than actions.

As you read Ezra's prayer in the margin, underline each time he used the word *guilt*.

How does Christianity offer freedom from guilt?
○ **By offering Jesus' blood as payment for sin**
○ **By requiring acts of devotion**
○ **By denying the existence of guilt**

Guilt, Ezra noted, is our response to our human nature. Guilt is universal. Because Jesus paid for our sin on the cross, we can be free of guilt. God's mercy alone allows us to stand in His presence.

The Desire for Legacy or Eternal Life

Every belief system seeks to give its followers the ability to leave something behind—a legacy that lasts beyond their mortal lifetimes. Even social clubs and civic groups understand the concept of legacy. People give to charities in memory of, or in honor of, loved ones. By doing so, they memorialize those persons' lives beyond their years.

Some years ago I attended a Universalist church on a Sunday evening to satisfy the requirements for a class in school. On that particular Sunday the congregation was dedicating a new library. This group, which does not believe in heaven or hell, salvation or sin, dedicated the library in memory of a deceased member. On a plaque the following words were inscribed: "In memory of _____, whose legacy far outlives his few years." Even pagans long for a legacy!

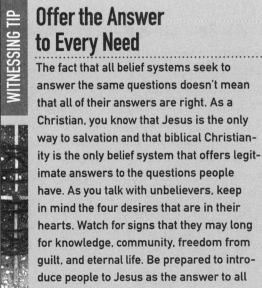

WITNESSING TIP

Offer the Answer to Every Need

The fact that all belief systems seek to answer the same questions doesn't mean that all of their answers are right. As a Christian, you know that Jesus is the only way to salvation and that biblical Christianity is the only belief system that offers legitimate answers to the questions people have. As you talk with unbelievers, keep in mind the four desires that are in their hearts. Watch for signs that they may long for knowledge, community, freedom from guilt, and eternal life. Be prepared to introduce people to Jesus as the answer to all of their needs.

" 'My God, I am ashamed and embarrassed to lift my face toward You, my God, because our iniquities are higher than our heads and our guilt is as high as the heavens. Our guilt has been terrible from the days of our fathers until the present. Because of our iniquities we have been handed over, along with our kings and priests, to the surrounding kings, and to the sword, captivity, plundering, and open shame, as it is today. ... After all that has happened to us because of our evil deeds and terrible guilt— though You, our God, have punished us less than our sins deserve and have allowed us to survive ... LORD God of Israel, You are righteous, for we survive as a remnant today. Here we are before You with our guilt, though no one can stand in Your presence because of this.' "
Ezra 9:6-7,13-15

The four religions we will study claim to offer hope for eternity. In Hinduism and Buddhism the concept of reincarnation grows from the desire for eternal life. If followers strive long enough and hard enough, they can achieve a perfection of sorts—nirvana. The final goal, nirvana, is a long-desired objective that ends the journey. In Islam heaven is seen as one hundred levels, and the level achieved is determined by the good works accomplished on earth. In modern Judaism the concept of rest and peace is seen in heavenly terms. According to modern Jewish scholars, once a Jewish person gets to heaven, he finally achieves tranquility, even though it eluded him on earth.

Christians hope for more than a meaningful legacy that is remembered on earth.

Read Jesus' words in the margin. Check the reason we can be confident about our hope for eternity.
○ **Our good works ensure a great reward.**
○ **Jesus promised that we will be with Him forever.**
○ **We should get every reward Jesus promised His disciples.**

Christians can rejoice in Jesus' promise that we will be with Him after death for eternity. That is a legacy that will last.

Fill in the blanks to identify the four needs every belief system tries to fulfill.
1. **The desire for _____**
2. **The desire for _____**
3. **The desire for freedom from _____**
4. **The desire for _____ or _____ _____**

Day 3: Four Categories of Religion

Desiring to ask Paul a specific question, the philosophers and skeptics "brought him to the Areopagus, and said, 'May we learn about this new teaching you're speaking of?' " (Acts 17:19). This question can be translated "Can you tell us what type of new teaching you're speaking of?" What is the difference? They were asking about the type of religion Paul described. The Greek is emphatic. The question would have sounded like "Can you please tell us—what in the world is this new teaching?"

Was Paul presenting a new god? Was he speaking of the lead god? Was this system of religion based on ethics and philosophy? Was it based on a human? Their question related to form or category.

All world religions fit into one of four categories: mythological, philosophical, empirical, or historical. When you talk with followers of other faiths, knowing the type of religion they follow will help you respond to their beliefs and questions.

" 'Your heart must not be troubled. Believe in God; believe also in Me. In My Father's hours are many dwelling places; if not, I would have told you. I am going away to prepare a place for you. If I go away and prepare a place for you, I will come back and receive you to Myself, so that where I am you may be also. You know the way where I am going.' "
John 14:1-4

Mythological Religions

A mythological belief system is based on a tale of supernatural proportions. For example, the Phoenecian god Baal, who is mentioned more than 90 times in the Bible, was a mythical god. The Canaanites also worshiped Baal as a god of the sun. Because he was the Canaanites' primary male god, he was believed to exist in various forms, though each one of these forms had a wife who was an exact replica of himself. As Elijah discovered in 1 Kings 18:25-29, the worship of Baal involved rituals in which the priests of Baal cut themselves and shouted. Observing this elaborate ceremony, which lasted for many hours, Elijah sarcastically advised the priests: " 'Shout loudly, for he's a god! Maybe he's thinking it over; maybe he has wandered away; or maybe he's on the road. Perhaps he's sleeping and will wake up!' " (1 Kings 18:27).

A mythological religion involves an otherworldly belief in systems or rituals that caused the god or gods to come to earth. This mentality requires a suspension of belief or rational logic, since believers must place their faith in a dimension they have never seen. For example, Muslims believe that on the Night of Power, Muhammed was whisked away to heaven and was carried around the world in an instant. Scientology is a contemporary example of a mythological religion.

Philosophical Religions

Perhaps it is unfair to refer to philosophies as religions, but certainly they meet the requirements we studied yesterday, offering answers to the need for knowledge, community, freedom from guilt, and legacy. These systems are probably better understood as ethical systems, based on knowledge and understanding. They usually do not involve a god per se but rather offer meaning in wisdom. In short, the more you know, the more religious you are. You become part of a secret band of the wise. You share in a knowledge of meaning and existence that the uninitiated can never grasp. An example of a philosophical religion is Marxism, which thrives among intellectuals on college and university campuses.

A philosophical system involves a degree of arrogance. If knowledge is salvation, then the teacher and mentor becomes a type of savior, leading followers to the truth. Thus, teachers serve in the position of priest. Their form of evangelism is argumentation. They reason you into understanding, usually by tearing apart your system.

The Bible mentions philosophical religions; for example, the Epicurean and Stoic philosophers we previously studied. Also consider Paul's admonition to the Colossian churches: "Therefore as you have received Christ Jesus the Lord, walk in Him, rooted and built up in Him and established in the faith, just as you were taught, and overflowing with thankfulness. Be careful that no one takes you captive through philosophy and empty deceit based on human tradition, based on the elemental forces of the world, and not based on Christ" (Col. 2:6-8).

Paul described the false teachers as deceitful, offering empty answers. This description reminds me of the college coffeehouse. No one on earth is as intelligent as first-year college students! Having taken one class in Western civilization or philosophy,

WITNESSING TIP

Ask Questions

In a culture of opinion, where everyone has an agenda and a cause, people are anxious to discuss their beliefs. Indeed, they long for the chance, and your own curiosity opens the door. Ask them what they believe. Ask them what holidays they observe, what their bumper stickers mean, and what their interests are. You would be amazed how many people are eager to have an audience! Later you can move to questions such as "Who is Jesus to you?" "What do you expect your faith to do for you?" and "What do you think causes evil and suffering in the world?" Ask questions, listen to the answers, and look for opportunities to present Christ.

they are ready to destroy every Christian they see!

Don't discount them because of their youth. And the nouveau piercings and cynicism can actually be a good thing. Their young minds, now engaged, are unwilling to believe something only because someone said it. If you can reach them with the truth of the gospel, young skeptics can become great soul-winners and apologists for Christ.

Empirical Religions

Empirical religions are based on proof. For groups like Universalists and Unitarians, any concept of salvation is based on knowledge, and the journey is more important than truth. These religions teach that contemplation and inquiry are more important than prayer, study is more important than belief, and knowledge is more important than faith. In an empirical religion, faith is the least of a follower's concerns.

Empiricists believe only what they can see, taste, touch, hear, and smell. Scientists and atheists often ask Christians whether events such as the resurrection can be submitted to scientific proof. What do we say to them?

The answer may surprise you. Using scientific methodology, you could not even prove the time you got up this morning! Science demands a controlled experiment with a control group and reproducible results. Can you go back in time? Of course not. History is proved not by scientific proof but by judicial evidence—oral testimony, written testimony, and physical evidence. Submit Christ's resurrection to those criteria. Does it pass the test?

Historical Religions

Historical religions are based on fact and faith at the same time. They are founded on literal persons who lived actual lives and taught concrete truths. For example, Buddhists revere the Buddha as a literal person. These belief systems rely on a tradition that has continued through time and is linked to actual events. Without these actual events or teachings, the religion has no validity.

In secular societies, historical religions can be seen as lineage. For example, someone is Jewish because his ancestors were Jewish. The religion is more a matter of heritage than of a belief system.

Match each religion with the correct definition.

___ 1. Mythological   a. Based on proof

___ 2. Philosophical   b. Based on fact and faith at the same time

___ 3. Empirical   c. Based on knowledge and understanding

___ 4. Historical   d. Based on a tale of supernatural proportions

What type of religion is Christianity? In truth, it has a basis in every category. We have supernatural (mythical) events, philosophical beliefs, empirical proof, and historical evidence. Perhaps that was Paul's point to the Colossians.

Read the verses in the margin. Then match the phrases with the categories of belief to indicate the way Christianity fits them all.

___ 1. Mythological   a. "who raised Him from the dead"

___ 2. Philosophical   b. "filled by Him"

___ 3. Empirical   c. "raised with Him through faith"

___ 4. Historical   d. "head over every ruler and authority"

"In Him the entire fullness of God's nature dwells bodily, and you have been filled by Him, who is the head over every ruler and authority. In Him you were also circumcised with a circumcision not done with hands, by putting off the body of flesh, in the circumcision of the Messiah. Having been buried with Him in baptism, you were also raised with Him through faith in the working of God, who raised Him from the dead."
Colossians 2:9-12

GLOBAL PERSPECTIVE

Paul Lived in a Religious Culture

Multiple Choices in the Apostle's Time:
• Emperor worship, mystery religions, philosophy, superstition
• Monotheism

Although Jewish, Paul still lived under the larger umbrella of the Roman Empire's religion. A virtual smorgasbord that adopted Greek gods and goddesses, mystery religions, philosophy, superstitions, and emperor worship offered Romans multiple religious choices. Seemingly, the older the religion, the more respect it received.

Romans freely mixed their own religious inclinations and traditions. Tolerance and multiple gods were the expected norm.

The lesser-educated emphasized superstitions; the better-educated accepted philosophy as a religion. Emperor worship was expected—but not uniformly enforced. The government offered the land and built temples to the gods. Everybody worshiped.

Only one theological issue stood at odds with Rome's religious stance—monotheism. Judaism was tolerated because of its long history. Yet an undercurrent of distrust between the Jews and the Romans was always present—a distrust that eventually erupted into bloodshed.

Eventually, thousands of Jews and Christians were martyred for their faith because they refused to worship pagan deities or to bow to the emperor as god.

G. B. Howell Jr.

In this passage Paul used all four types of religious systems to prove the validity of Christianity:

- The mythological, or supernatural, is found in the phrase "filled by Him" (b). A Christian's filling cannot be seen with the eyes. It is a supernatural dimension of salvation.
- Christianity is also a philosophical system, as expressed in the phrase "head over every ruler and authority" (d). Christ is head over all.
- Christianity provides empirical proof: we were "raised with Him through faith" (c). Our faith is evidence of Christ's presence in us. Believers become part of the oral testimony about Christ's purpose in our lives.
- Historical evidence is represented in the phrase "who raised Him from the dead" (a). Jesus' bodily resurrection actually happened in history.

Day 4: The Worldview of the Skeptics

In addition to the objections of the Epicurean and Stoic philosophers, Paul's teaching in Athens elicited another response from his audience: " 'What you say sounds strange to us, and we want to know what these ideas mean' " (Acts 17:20). What was Paul teaching that was so strange to the Athenian philosophers? The word *strange* is from the Greek term *xenizo*, which is usually translated *novel* or *surprising*. However, it is also the term for visitors who come to our homes by surprise. For instance, it is found in Hebrews 13:2: "Do not neglect to show hospitality to strangers, for by this some have entertained angels without knowing it" (NASB). Conversely, someone who is afraid of foreigners is xenophobic.

How does this understanding flavor the translation? The philosophers seemed to suggest that Paul's teaching took them by surprise. He was preaching a doctrine that was foreign to their ears, and this was the first time they had entertained the notion of a God who took on flesh and conquered death. Today we would call these men skeptics.

The skeptical and the atheistic cultural worlds are the same. Skeptics are not necessarily atheists but rather more agnostic. Like atheists, skeptics are unwilling to commit to any system or to disavow any.

When confronted with the message of Jesus Christ, skeptics and atheists reject it because it contradicts their presuppositions. A presupposition is an assumption. When skeptics enter a debate, they base their arguments on

CULTURE CLASH

The Newest Minority?

Ellen Johnson, president of American Atheists, an organization founded by Madalyn Murray O'Hair in 1963, fears that discrimination against atheists might be legal, despite the Civil Rights Act that bans discrimination on the basis of religion. "I want to be protected as an atheist. I don't want to say that I'm religious in order to have my rights protected," Johnson says.[3]

assumptions that may or may not be true. You may hear a skeptic make a statement like "Of course, no one believes in heaven" or "Creation by a Supreme Being cannot be validated." If you dissect the presuppositions, you have made great strides toward reaching skeptics for Christ. Let's examine a few of those presuppositions.

Skeptics Assume That All Belief Systems Are Equally Wrong

A skeptic begins with the assumption that all systems of faith are wrong. Some believe these systems originated from a need to create a mythology, while others assume that science replaced religion. Religion, they submit, was invented to provide answers. When science actually discovered the answers to the great questions of life, existence, and the world, religion became outdated.

The problem is that although science attempts to answer the how questions, it is unable to answer the why questions.

Examine the chart "Unanswered Questions of Science" on this page. Place an S beside the questions science tries to answer. Place an F beside the questions only the Christian faith can answer.

___ Why did the world begin?   **___ What is the purpose of life?**
___ How did the world begin?   **___ How can life be deepened?**
___ What is the process of life?   **___ How can life be lengthened?**

Unanswered Questions of Science	
Questions Science Tries to Answer	**Questions Science Ignores**
The origin of life	The meaning of life
How we got here	Why we are here
The Big Bang theory of explosion	Who started the Big Bang
How we coexist through human history	Why we coexist through human history
How we can use scientific and medical procedures	Whether we should use all scientific and medical procedures

Science tries to explain how the world began but not why. Science attempts to explain the process of life but not its purpose. Science strives to lengthen life with medicine but cannot deepen life. Ask a skeptic to explain the origins of the universe, and he will speak for hours. Ask him to explain the meaning of life, and he is mute.

Only biblical faith can explain some things.

Skeptics Assume That Faith and Reason Are Mutually Exclusive

Norman Geisler once cowrote a book titled *I Don't Have Enough Faith to Be an Atheist*, in which he, along with other authors, made a strong case for this simple idea: it takes faith to be an atheist! Think about it. You have to believe that the Big Bang happened spontaneously. You must have faith that science will eventually discover proof for the evolutionary hypothesis.

Evolution teaches that humans slowly developed from primate species over the course of millions or billions of years. Yet scientists have never discovered a single piece of evidence that one species evolved into another. They bombard various species and insects with X-rays and gamma rays, and they produce insects that mutate into various forms. They get flies with many wings, few wings, and no wings. Yet they have never been able to turn the fly into a caterpillar or a hummingbird.

Although no substantial proof exists to support evolution, scientists and skeptics alike continue to assume that it is true. Sounds like they operate on faith as well, doesn't it? Conversely, biblical faith acknowledges the legitimacy of human discovery through scientific research. Christians believe that the world operates on reasonable laws of nature that were originally established by a reasonable God.

"From the creation of the world His [God's] invisible attributes, that is, His eternal power and divine nature, have been clearly seen, being understood through what He has made."
Romans 1:20

Read the verse in the margin and identify two ways God is revealed in His creation.

1. _____

2. _____

> **WITNESSING TIP**
>
> ## Prepare a Reasonable Defense
>
> Skeptics claim to place reason above faith. To witness to a skeptic, take a thoughtful, reasoned approach. Start by listening to his ideas. You may discover that he doesn't know exactly what he believes. Show that you care about him and accept him even though you do not agree with his beliefs. Present logical arguments for your belief in God, Jesus, and biblical truth. Discuss why you believe Christianity is a credible belief system, providing biblical support and refuting the presuppositions of atheism. Such an approach will require advance preparation on your part.

Both nature and human beings reveal God's handiwork. Christians don't ignore the truth revealed by science, but we aren't foolish enough to think that science is all we need to know.

Skeptics Assume That Faith Is Weakness

A famous American once called Christians weak because we "lean on Jesus like a crutch." Certainly we lean on Jesus Christ. However, everyone leans on something. Humanity's nature is to rely on external strength. Some depend on drugs. Others crave cigarettes or alcohol. Still others find purpose in hobbies, sports, or entertainment.

Because this tendency is a universal condition, it isn't weakness. It is evidence of being human. Even those who boastfully say they rely on no one or nothing rely on their own strength. The very fact that they get tired and weak shows that even they must rely on something—in this case, rest and relaxation. Others might rely on their jobs or cunning to provide them with a sense of accomplishment. Does that make them weak as well?

Read "The Christian Worldview" on this page. Does leaning on Jesus make you weaker or stronger? ○ **Weaker** ○ **Stronger**

How? _____

_____

_____

_____

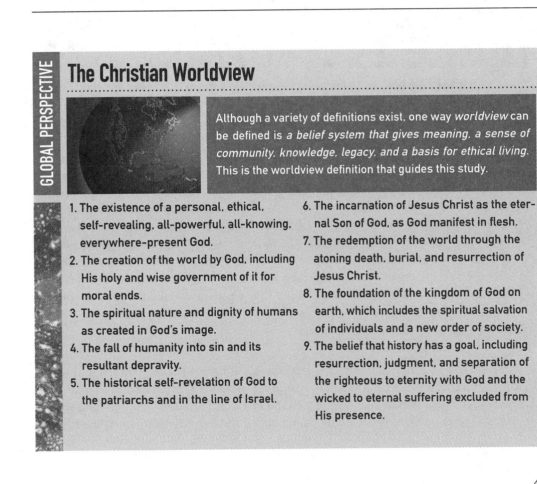

GLOBAL PERSPECTIVE

The Christian Worldview

Although a variety of definitions exist, one way *worldview* can be defined is *a belief system that gives meaning, a sense of community, knowledge, legacy, and a basis for ethical living.* This is the worldview definition that guides this study.

1. The existence of a personal, ethical, self-revealing, all-powerful, all-knowing, everywhere-present God.
2. The creation of the world by God, including His holy and wise government of it for moral ends.
3. The spiritual nature and dignity of humans as created in God's image.
4. The fall of humanity into sin and its resultant depravity.
5. The historical self-revelation of God to the patriarchs and in the line of Israel.
6. The incarnation of Jesus Christ as the eternal Son of God, as God manifest in flesh.
7. The redemption of the world through the atoning death, burial, and resurrection of Jesus Christ.
8. The foundation of the kingdom of God on earth, which includes the spiritual salvation of individuals and a new order of society.
9. The belief that history has a goal, including resurrection, judgment, and separation of the righteous to eternity with God and the wicked to eternal suffering excluded from His presence.

Day 5: The Worldview of the Spiritualist

I love the parenthetical sentence Luke inserted in Acts 17:21: "Now all the Athenians and the foreigners residing there spent their time on nothing else but telling or hearing something new." You can almost hear the sarcasm in his voice as he dryly stated that the philosophers spent most of their days attempting to come up with a new thought or revelation to impress the others. The adjective new comes from the Greek word *kainos,* which means *unused, unheard,* and *fresh.* The philosophers were obsessed with the BBT—the bigger and better thing.

Our secular culture is also driven by this need. The products we buy are advertised as new and improved. We want the newest electronics or computers. We shop for the latest fashion trends. In fact, like the Athenians, we are drawn to anything that sounds, looks, or smells like a fresh perspective, concept, or product.

GLOBAL PERSPECTIVE

Political Correctness

The phrase *political correctness* can be found as far back as a 1793 U.S. Supreme Court decision, but did not take on its current significance until late in the 20th century.

An online encyclopedia describes political correctness as "the attempted erection of boundaries or limits to language, the range of acceptable public debate, and conduct." In its most common usage, it describes the altering of language or terminology for the purpose of eliminating offensive or objectionable words or stereotypes, frequently in regard to an individual or group's race, gender, disability, or another characteristic.

Efforts to be politically correct frequently emphasize being inoffensive at the expense of honesty or truth. The idea of aborting a baby creates mental pain, so the colder, harsher, less-cuddly term *fetus* is used. A homosexual takes offense at being told his chosen lifestyle is sinful; political correctness refers to his sexual orientation, implying a condition beyond his control.

Society also applies political correctness to religion. So as not to offend individuals from various religious backgrounds, political correctness says we must accept all religions and all beliefs as equally valid and worthy. When the Christian community speaks of Jesus as the only way to God or of the need for all to come to salvation through Christ, political correctness attempts to step in and rule the message out of order.[4]

The same is true of America's spiritual landscape. Not only is every traditional world religion represented in our nation, but a number of prevalent philosophies also have their own set of beliefs that they vaguely characterize as spiritual. They share a worldview we call spiritualism. A decidedly vague belief system, spiritualism is based on a faith in otherworldly influences. It has its roots in earth-centered emotional experiences and cloudy, noncreedal, and nondogmatic beliefs or feelings.

Spiritualistic philosophies differ from the worldview of the skeptic in this respect: *Skeptics assume that everyone is wrong. Spiritualists assume that everyone is right.*

Thus, a spiritualist believes his truth may contradict your truth, but both are valid. In our culture we are surrounded by people who feel that the only heresy is to believe in heresy! As long as you are willing to say that every system is valid and true, you are welcome to play along. However, if you believe that Christ alone is Lord, then you are put in the crosshairs of their scorn. What, then, do spiritualists believe?

Spiritualists Accept All Religions as Being of Human Origin: Humanism

Spiritualists are not concerned with the foundations of your faith; they are just thrilled you are a person of faith. They believe that everyone is searching and that everyone has a journey. A popular television personality regularly speaks of the inner light each person possesses.

This is a form of humanism. Humanism is a system of beliefs that are either human-centered or human-inspired. The idea of God or gods is considered superstition. Humans are capable of solving their own problems and finding their own truth. Instead of looking to God and His truth revealed in Scripture, all people find their own truths and answers, and no one has the right to say their truth is better than anyone else's.

Spiritualists Accept All Religions as the Same: Relativism

Spiritualists believe that all systems somehow spring from the same source. Because all religions seek the same goals—answers, peace, belonging, hope—they must all come from the same place. A relativist would say that it doesn't matter what you believe as long as you believe something.

Spiritualists Accept All Religions as True: Syncretism

The third principle espoused is the belief that all religions and systems are equally true. Often a syncretist uses the analogy of the blind men and the elephant to describe this conviction. Imagine three blind men approaching an elephant. One grabs the tail, one grabs the tusk, and the third one grabs the ear. Each struggles to describe the elephant by using his personal experience. One speaks of the sharp horn of the tusk. The second one describes the long, ropelike tail. The third depicts a floppy, leathery ear. Each man is truthfully describing the part of the elephant he has experienced.

This, spiritualists conclude, is the reason for the differences in world religions. Each one is right in its description because each one describes its experience. Those descriptions may have contradicted one another but only inasmuch as they held a different part of the same elephant. Christianity, Islam, Buddhism, Hinduism, and Judaism, spiritualists deduce, are all properly correct and, at the same time, only partially correct.

DEFINITION

Spiritualism

A vague belief system based on faith in other-worldly influence. It has its roots in earth-centered emotional experiences and cloudy, noncreedal, and nondogmatic beliefs or feelings.

Syncretism

A belief that all religions are part of the same system. Being religious is the common denominator. The names of gods, the sacred books, and the rituals may be different, but everyone believes basically the same thing. In our modern context this view predominates.

Also see the definitions of *humanism, relativism,* and *existentialism* on pages 35–36.

Spiritualists Accept All Religions as Helpful: Existentialism

The final belief of our spiritualist culture is a pragmatic belief. Existentialism teaches that if something works for you, it is true for you. You have experienced this truth, and it changed you. As long as your success is heartfelt, existentialists believe, it is valid.

Match each spiritualist belief with the answer it offers for spiritual meaning.

___ **1. Humanism**   **a. Believe in everything.**
___ **2. Relativism**   **b. Believe in your ability.**
___ **3. Syncretism**   **c. Believe in whatever works.**
___ **4. Existentialism**   **d. Believe in something.**

Although the beliefs of a spiritualist worldview are somewhat nebulous, the implications of these beliefs are quite serious. Humanism means that you believe in your ability (b). Therefore, people are the center of religion, not God. Relativism says to believe in something (d). Therefore, faith is more important than the object of your faith. Syncretism encourages people to believe in everything (a). Therefore, all religions come from the same source and lead to the same result. Existentialism teaches a belief in whatever works (c). Therefore, truth is entirely personal. What is true for you may not be true for me.

How would you respond to the spiritualist claim that truth is relative and that all faiths are equally valid?

_____

Christianity vigorously contradicts spiritualist teachings because of this fundamental distinction: Jesus alone is the Truth. He alone is the Path. He alone is the Door. It is impossible to reconcile His claims with spiritualist teachings. Jesus made it plain: " 'I am the way, the truth, and the life. No one comes to the Father except through Me' " (John 14:6).

WITNESSING TIP

Assert Absolute Truth

Prayer is extremely important in seeking to influence a spiritualist. With love and assurance, demonstrate that the spiritualist perspective is self-contradictory. The assertion that there is no absolute truth is itself a statement of absolute truth. Confidently assert that truth has an objective basis. Point to the historical facts about Christ's life, death, and resurrection, which confirm His identity as the way, the truth, and the life.

[1] www.adherents.com/Na/Na_173.html, Zuckerman.

[2] H. Richard Niebuhr, *Christ and Culture* (New York: Harper and Row, 1975).

[3] Doron Taussig, "Losing Your Religion," *Philadelphia City Paper* [online], 24–30 March 2005 [cited 2 May 2005]. Available from the Internet: *www.citypaper.net.*

[4] "Political Correctness," *Wikipedia: The Free Encyclopedia* [online, cited 30 April 2005]. Available from the Internet: *www.en.wikipedia.org.*

Viewer Guide
Group Session 2

Review Segment: Politically Correct, Biblically Corrupt

When Paul preached at the Areopagus, the Supreme Court of Athens,
he presented _____.

All systems deal with these eternal questions:

* How do I find _____?

* How do I find _____?

* How do I find _____?

* How do I find _____?

* How do I live beyond _____?

* Is this life the _____?

This study is about presenting _____ in a variety of ways, to a variety of
people who need _____ just as much as you did.

Teaching Segment: A Not-So-Brave New World

In a politically correct culture, the only heresy is to believe in _____.

They don't want to reject Jesus or mock Him; they want to _____ Him.
All four major systems and this culture have found a way to approach Jesus by
_____ Jesus.

In this new politically correct world, if you take a stand for anything, you
_____ something. Their one absolute is there are no _____.

If Jesus is the way, everything else is _____.
It's not that we're _____ anyone; we're trying to _____ everyone
to Him as Lord.

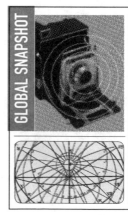

3 A Not-So-Brave New World

The Gospel According to the Global Culture

Paul stood in the middle of the Areopagus and said: "Men of Athens! I see that you are extremely religious in every respect. For as I was passing through and observing the objects of your worship, I even found an altar on which was inscribed: TO AN UNKNOWN GOD. Therefore, what you worship in ignorance, this I proclaim to you. The God who made the world and everything in it—He is Lord of heaven and earth and does not live in shrines made by hands. Neither is He served by human hands, as though He needed anything, since He Himself gives everyone life and breath and all things. From one man He has made every nation of men to live all over the earth and has determined their appointed times and the boundaries of where they live, so that they might seek God, and perhaps they might reach out and find Him, though He is not far from each one of us. For in Him we live and move

THIS WEEK'S GOAL

No.3

After this week's study you will be able to—
- give biblical answers to five worldview questions;
- identify four ways world religions attempt to mold Jesus in a new image;
- use Paul's speech in Acts 17:22-34 to refute false views of Jesus.

and exist, as even some of your own poets have said, 'For we are also His offspring.' Being God's offspring, then, we shouldn't think that the divine nature is like gold or silver or stone, an image fashioned by human art and imagination.

"Therefore, having overlooked the times of ignorance, God now commands all people everywhere to repent, because He has set a day on which He is going to judge the world in righteousness by the Man He has appointed. He has provided proof of this to everyone by raising Him from the dead."

When they heard about resurrection of the dead, some began to ridicule him. But others said, "We will hear you about this again." So Paul went out from their presence. However, some men joined him and believed, among whom were Dionysius the Areopagite, a woman named Damaris, and others with them. Acts 17:22-34

A Schizophrenic Christ

The images on the video are somewhat hazy, but events are unmistakable. Two men, hands bound, are silently led into a city square. The city is obviously Middle Eastern, and every person standing within camera range is wearing Islamic clothing. Four men begin digging a hole, approximately three feet deep, while another group of men unroll two long, white sacks. The two bound men, obviously criminals, quietly stand with their heads lowered.

Once the sacks are unrolled, the men are placed feet first into the closed end, and the muslin-type material is gathered over their heads and tied. The leaders of the group order the men to be lowered into the two parallel holes. Rocks and dirt are shoveled into the hole and stomped flat. In the bright sun, viewers can see the outlines of the two men through the cloth, and their hands are clasped as if in prayer.

The camera now cuts to a Muslim woman in a studio. She is wearing the traditional *hijab,* so only her face is visible, but she speaks clearly as she reads the indictment. Even a viewer who doesn't speak Arabic can ascertain that she is pronouncing judgment on the two men, and with a measure of finality she concludes her reading.

The scene changes back to the city square, where a crowd gathers around the two white bags. With horror you watch as men begin to pick up rocks. Then a rock flies through the air, bouncing off the head of one of the men. A barrage of rocks immediately follows, as every male in the village, young and old, flings stone missiles at the two convicted men.

Though the entire scene lasts only about eight minutes, it moves at an excruciating pace. The two figures slump to the ground, and the once-white sheets are now stained a dark crimson. Within minutes both men are dead.

This sobering scene is not from a movie; it is a real stoning that was broadcast across this particular Islamic country by satellite. The time stamp at the bottom of the screen also reveals that the execution took place just a few years ago. However, the time stamp does not tell the entire story. The two men were executed for the sole crime of becoming Christians. The men, new believers in Jesus Christ, were praying as they prepared to join their Savior.

Is Sharing God's Love Terrorism?

One local newspaper carried a story about an organized, community-wide, door-to-door effort by Southern Baptists to take the good news of Jesus' gift of salvation to as many people as possible. In response to the news, one writer to the newspaper stated: "This is religious tyranny and terrorism at its worst. I fear these people every bit as much as I would fear Osama bin Laden."[2]

Now contrast that scene with this one. A large evangelical church in the Midwest has invited a Muslim *imam* (pastor) to speak in its pulpit. He rises to the pulpit to address the congregation and states: "I am honored to be here with you. You see, Muslims believe in Jesus. We believe in Jesus perhaps even more than you do. We worship the same God. ..."

Do those two scenes fit? If Muslims and Christians in fact worshiped the same God and believed in the same Jesus, why would 30 Islamic countries make conversion to Christianity a capital offense? If we worshiped the same Christ, why would such videotapes exist, and why would such scenes be possible?

The Jesus of whom Muslims speak was a prophet who served Allah and spoke of the coming of Muhammed. The Islamic Jesus (*Isa* in Arabic) was never crucified and will return to marry, teach, and die. Then he will be buried next to Abu Bakr, a Muslim leader who came after Muhammed.

This Jesus is certainly not the Savior we see in Scripture. In a global culture Christians are now confronted with a relatively new phenomenon: a modified Jesus. Every world religion and cultural movement now attempts to mold Jesus to fit its worldview. These belief systems no longer reject Him, but neither do they accept Him as the God-Man, Redeemer, and second Person of the Trinity. We live in a confused world that presents a schizophrenic Christ.

If there is any comfort for Christians who attempt to share the gospel in such a culture, it is that the early Christians also faced such a world. Paul stood in the face of contradictory Roman mythologies and clearly presented Christ as Lord. How was Paul able to defeat such a baffling set of systems? He was effective because he understood their doctrines.

Effective Christian witnesses are able to reach others because they not only understand their own faith but also have a working knowledge of other belief systems. They anticipate the objections they face because they understand the assumptions by which other people live. As you study this week, ask God to help you learn the assumptions and misconceptions of other belief systems. Observe the way Paul masterfully dissected the philosophies of his audience and confronted their halfhearted respect for Christ. Understanding the mind-set of the other faiths is the line that separates frustrated believers and those who flourish in today's pluralistic environment.

Day 1: Worldview Questions

As Paul began his address in Acts 17, he was already operating from a disadvantage. As we studied last week, the philosophers already had preconceived notions about him. They already disliked him. The dialogue prior to Paul's sermon left little room for debate: [18]"Some of the Epicurean and Stoic philosophers argued with him. Some said, 'What is this pseudo-intellectual trying to say?' Others replied, 'He seems to be a preacher of foreign deities'—because he was telling the good news about Jesus and the resurrection. [19]They took him and brought him to the Areopagus, and said, 'May we learn about this new teaching you're speaking of? [20]For what you say sounds strange to us, and we want to know what these ideas mean' " (Acts 17:18-20).

What clues do you see in these verses that indicate the philosophers disliked Paul and his message?

_____

Have you ever been in a setting where you sensed that everyone disliked you because you are a Christian?   ○ Yes ○ No   **If so, describe how you felt.**

_____

The Apostle Paul certainly understood that scenario. The philosophers were arguing with Paul (v. 18,) called him a pseudo-intellectual (v. 18), assumed he was preaching a new god (v. 18), and called his teaching strange (v. 20).

Pseudo-intellectual is an interesting term in the Greek language. Transliterated *spermologos*, the word appears only here in the Bible. It is a metaphor that literally means *picking up seed*. It carries the imagery of a crow picking up random grains of seed in the fields. The picture is that of a buffoon who scrounges around the marketplace, taking anything he can find on the ground.

Does this insight change the way you read that verse? Perhaps you had assumed that those who asked Paul about the gospel were sincere, but the text does not support that assumption. Instead, you can almost hear the sneering sarcasm of the philosophers. Seeing Paul as a lunatic, they thought this would be entertaining.

If you were seeking to witness to a group of people and they treated you with open derision, how would you respond?

_____

_____

Paul used their disparagement to his advantage: " 'Men of Athens! I see that you are extremely religious in every respect' " (Acts 17:22). To offset their skepticism, Paul began his address by appealing to the single unifying factor in Athens: everyone was religious. As in our culture today, it was fashionable to be spiritual and religious.

Which of the following characteristics fit the people today who consider themselves spiritual while rejecting historic Christian beliefs?
○ **1. Spiritualists are human-centered in their beliefs.**
○ **2. Spiritualists view all religious beliefs as equally true.**
○ **3. Spiritualists believe that Jesus is the only way to salvation.**
○ **4. Spiritualists believe that all religions come from the same source and lead to the same result.**
○ **5. Spiritualists seek a relationship with the personal God of the Bible.**
○ **6. Spiritualists reject absolutes; truth is whatever works.**

Please don't make the mistake of confusing spiritual and religious people with Christians! They are radically and eternally different. Our modern spiritualism is a trendy, vague movement, thriving on a buffet-style approach to religion and ritual. It embraces everything and nothing at the same moment. It embraces everything because it heavily borrows from all religions and world systems. It embraces nothing because the only absolute in the world of spiritualism is the complete elimination of absolutes. You should have checked all of the statements except 3 and 5. ·

CULTURE CLASH

Do-It-Yourself Faith

Paul Naras gives an insider's perspective on the new spirituality or New Age: "It is a human potential movement. ... The new age movement is shapeless and indeterminate. ... It celebrates diversity of thought and conclusion. ... Its devotees will be embracing the 'master Within.' ... Faith is not extinct. It has simply been remolded. ... There will be few (if any) official manifestos or commandments since the bedrock of New consciousness will be engineered on personal creativity, accountability and integrity."[3]

Like our present culture, Paul's audience was spiritual and mystical. In fact, the term Paul used for *religious* (*deisidaimonia*) indicated that his listeners were almost obsessively superstitious. Whether they worshiped Diana, Zeus, or their ancestors, they yearned for a relationship with something beyond themselves. This basic need that unifies humanity is a tremendous insight by Paul that allowed him to appeal to his listeners' common desires and shared questions.

Paul's approach is a wonderful example for us. Every human being in every region of the earth longs to answer fundamental questions about life. We have identified five worldview questions as our focus in weeks 4–7:

1. *Who am I?* The questions of God and humanity
2. *How can I know?* The questions of authority and truth
3. *Why am I here?* The questions of purpose and ethics
4. *Where am I going?* The questions of eternity and legacy
5. *Is there any hope?* The questions of salvation and security

These questions are universal. Even atheists, who do not like why questions, must grudgingly find a purpose for their existence!

Review Acts 17:22-34 on pages 50–51 and match each worldview question with Paul's masterful answer.

___ **1. Who am I?**

___ **2. How can I know?**

___ **3. Why am I here?**

___ **4. Where am I going?**

___ **5. Is there any hope?**

a. **"... so that they might seek God, and perhaps they might reach out and find Him."**

b. **"He has set a day on which He is going to judge the world in righteousness."**

c. **"The God who made the world and everything in it—He is Lord of heaven and earth." "In Him we live and move and exist."**

d. **"God now commands all people everywhere to repent."**

e. **"He has provided proof of this to everyone by raising Him from the dead."**

As we discussed last week, asking questions is a brilliant method for sharing the gospel. We live in an era when everyone wants to be heard. Why do you think reality shows dominate every television channel? People are willing to do disgusting and embarrassing things on television because they are desperate to be famous! Beneath the activist bumper stickers that cover car windows, below the screaming hordes of protestors carrying interchangeable signs, and behind every reality-show failure beats the heart of a desperate person who longs to know the peace that comes only through faith in Jesus Christ.

WITNESSING TIP

Challenge Assumptions

The fundamental problem in presenting the gospel in our culture is that virtually every lost person already has a predetermined misunderstanding about Christ. Because every belief system now attempts to construct a Jesus who matches its philosophy, we must learn to present the biblical Jesus in absolutely clear terms. When Paul addressed the philosophers in Acts 17, he not only presented the gospel but also rejected their false arguments. Paul demonstrated an important principle of biblical salvation: before people can be saved, they must first recognize they are lost. Turning to Christ also involves a total rejection of past beliefs.

You could have answered the activity above in more than one way, but my responses were 1. c, 2. e, 3. a, 4. b, 5. d.

Review the five worldview questions by completing the following.

1. Who _____ _____?

2. How can I _____?

3. Why am I _____?

4. Where am I _____?

5. Is there any _____?

Day 2: Redefining Jesus as a Prophet

Many religious systems are willing to include Jesus among their beliefs as long as they can construct Him into a form they can accept. Paul encountered the same practice among the religions of Athens.

" 'As I was passing through and observing the objects of your worship, I even found an altar on which was inscribed: TO AN UNKNOWN GOD. There-fore, what you worship in ignorance, this I proclaim to you. The God who made the world and everything in it—He is Lord of heaven and earth and does not live in shrines made by hands. Neither is He served by human hands, as though He needed anything, since He Himself gives everyone life and breath and all things.'" Acts 17:23-25

Read Acts 17:23-25 in the margin. Match the statements about the way the Athenians revered Jesus with the evidence Paul presented.

___ 1. They gave Him a name.

___ 2. They put Him alongside the other gods.

___ 3. They were willing to worship Him.

a. Altar
b. Unknown
c. Objects

WITNESSING TIP

Proclaim Jesus as the One and Only

When other belief systems claim that Jesus is just a prophet or a teacher, they deny His uniqueness as God's Son. Use John 3:16 to emphasize that Jesus is the unique Son of God. The phrase "One and Only" in that verse is a translation of the Greek term meaning *unique, one of a kind.* Jesus was much more than a prophet. Explain that He is God incarnate, the one and only Son of God; that He is the only Christ; and that we can have a personal relationship with Him through faith. Testify about your personal relationship with Jesus Christ and the difference He makes in your life. Make sure your life testifies to the change that has taken place because of your faith.

The Athenians were willing to worship Jesus; they had built an altar for Him. They gave Him a name ("UNKNOWN"). They had even put Him alongside the other gods, or objects. The Athenians had no problem showing reverence to Jesus as long as they did not have to abandon their other idols. They wanted to cover all their bases, so in lieu of knowing Him personally by name, they simply marked one god "UNKNOWN."

Does such a teaching sound farfetched or rare? Sadly, it is not. The world's religions and spiritualists today attempt to reduce Jesus to the status of a great teacher or prophet. Regardless of the system or politics of the group, they all attempt to redefine Jesus in their own terms.

Think about non-Christians you know. What do they believe about Jesus?
○ **An insane Mediterranean peasant**
○ **A moral teacher**
○ **A prophet who heralded the coming of a greater leader**
○ **A creation of the Christian church**
○ **Other:** _____

The vast majority of unbelievers respect Jesus as a prophet or teacher. They may intellectually accept that He actually lived in history, said He was God, and was crucified. Yet they are not saved.

Our culture does not reject Jesus as much as it simply pays Him deference as a great teacher. They hold Him in great regard and may even attempt to tell you how much they esteem Him and appreciate His teachings. They show consideration for Him only as one part of the whole or as one voice among many.

Paul firmly responded to the Athenians' desire to make Jesus merely a prophet.

What did Paul call Jesus in the passage you read in the margin on page 56?
○ **One of many spiritual leaders**
○ **The greatest teacher of all**
○ **Lord of heaven and earth**
○ **Someone who attained divinity through self-realization**

Paul called Jesus "Lord of heaven and earth" (Acts 17:24). He wasn't willing to allow Jesus to be reduced to one part of a system or one of many gods. Christ is Lord, and He gives everyone life.

The terms Paul used to describe Jesus and the pagan idols illustrate a two-pronged approach of discrediting the false gods and declaring Jesus' deity. Paul used the word *sebasma* to indicate that the objects of the Athenians' worship were literally false idols (see Acts 17:23). Not only is God the true God; everything else is a so-called god.

In contrast, Paul used the unequivocal word *Lord* for Jesus. The Greek word *kurios* designates absolute supremacy and rule. Jesus is the sovereign Possessor and Owner of both the heavens (*ouranos*) and the earth. Not only was Paul unambiguous about Jesus, but he was also provocative. By stating that Jesus is Lord, Paul both exalted Christ and declared all other gods to be false.

What means have you used to show people that their self-styled versions of Christ are false gods?

_____

How have you tried to show them Jesus' true identity? _____

Day 3: Realigning Jesus as a Partner

While I was in Israel in 1994, I was walking the streets of Jerusalem and entered a small store hoping to find a soft drink. The man working behind the counter took me by surprise. He looked like me in virtually every detail. His eyes, his build, and even his haircut made me feel as if I were looking in a mirror. Even though he spoke very little English, we exchanged a laugh. It was obvious that we both saw the striking similarities.

The German word *doppelgänger* means *a ghostly double of a living person.* Historically, the word referred to a mystical appearance of the undead or a harbinger of imminent danger. Although the *doppelgänger* looks like someone, he is essentially, personally, and functionally different.

When you hear the modern media and culture describe Jesus, you might wonder whether He has a *doppelgänger*. They speak of Him in respectful terms, but you realize that they are not describing the Jesus of the Bible. Instead of defining Him as the Lord of heaven and earth, as Paul preached in Acts 17:24, they present Jesus as one of many lords or gods.

The central difference between this method and yesterday's method can be expressed this way:

CULTURE CLASH

Makeovers of Jesus

Several groups in our culture try to make a partner of Jesus.

- Some make Jesus their spokesman, as if He were a celebrity endorser bringing His divine seal of approval to their agenda. Examples: the "Jesus the vegetarian" and "Jesus the environmentalist" movements.
- Some make Jesus part of their board of directors, as if He were one of many representatives of their system. He is viewed as one among equals.
- Some attempt to give Jesus a celebrity makeover by dressing Him in their garb. Example: the "Jesus was a homosexual" movement reads into Scripture (eisegesis) and makes assumptions in an attempt to force Jesus into that camp.

Such groups use Jesus to meet their temporary wants rather than their eternal needs. This is the political rather than the spiritual Jesus.

> *Those who redefine Jesus as only a prophet seek to lower Him to the level of other teachers and guides. Those who realign Jesus as a partner seek to raise other teachers to His level.*

When you talk with a skeptic, he may begin by referring to Jesus as a mere prophet. However, if you can show him that the Bible clearly presents Jesus as Lord, he may turn to this form of reasoning:

> *You say that the Bible calls Jesus Lord. We say that He is one of many lords.*

This reasoning seeks to include Jesus with many other exalted gods in a given belief system. As you will discover in weeks 4 and 5, this view of Jesus represents a marked distinction between Hinduism and Buddhism. Hinduism accepts many gods and is therefore willing to bring Jesus alongside these gods. Buddhism, on the other hand, denies the existence of any personal deity, so Buddhists are more comfortable lowering Jesus to a teacher or prophet.

Explain how the effort to realign Jesus as partner denies His true identity.

_____

_____

_____

Paul would not allow the Athenians to reshape Jesus.

Read in the margin Paul's words to the Athenians and underline phrases that emphasize Christ's uniqueness. Then check your answers as you read the following discussion of Paul's arguments.

Paul used several arguments to present a case that Jesus alone is Lord of the world.

The Argument from Creation
Paul presented God as the sole Creator: " 'From one man He has made every nation of men' " (Acts 17:26). All people in every nation owe their existence to the God of the Bible. Even though Greek and Roman mythology offered their own theories of creation, Paul disputed them. In one succinct sentence Paul affirmed the biblical Adam ("one man"), the universal relationship of people ("every nation"), and God alone as the Creator ("He").

Other New Testament texts clearly include Jesus in the creation account, indicating that He was intimately involved in forming our universe (see Col. 1:13-17).

WITNESSING TIP

Show That Jesus Is Lord

Use Paul's arguments in Acts 17:26-29 to show a lost person that Jesus alone is Lord of the world:
- *The argument from creation.* Show that God lovingly created the lost person with a unique identity and purpose.
- *The argument from sovereignty.* Show that God orchestrated events in the person's life to lead to the opportunity to enter a fulfilling love relationship with Him.
- *The argument from universal need.* Show that a relationship with God through Christ meets every need in the person's life, especially the need to overcome sin and death and to have abundant, eternal life.

" 'From one man He has made every nation of men to live all over the earth and has determined their appointed times and the boundaries of where they live, so that they might seek God, and perhaps they might reach out and find Him, though He is not far from each one of us. For in Him we live and move and exist, as even some of your own poets have said, "For we are also His offspring." Being God's offspring, then, we shouldn't think that the divine nature is like gold or silver or stone, an image fashioned by human art and imagination.' "
Acts 17:26-29

The Argument from Sovereignty

Paul emphasized God's sovereignty over all humanity: " 'He ... has determined their appointed times and the boundaries of where they live' " (Acts 17:26). Paul clearly stated that the biblical God controls not only the length of our lives ("appointed times") but also the very geography and ethnic background of our lives ("boundaries"). No human-divine cooperation is involved here. God did this alone.

This statement also applies to our universal brotherhood. Because God created us all and we all came from one man, we are all part of a divine family with a common Father and Creator. Certainly Paul believed that we are all equal before God and equally created. Each man and woman is on spiritually level ground and is therefore a prospect for salvation.

The Argument from Universal Need

Paul took an interesting approach in Acts 17:28, using a pagan writer of antiquity to present Christ: " 'In Him we live and move and exist, as even some of your own poets have said, "For we are also His offspring." ' " Quoting the poet Aratus, Paul pointed the philosophers to all people's yearning to have a relationship with their Creator.

Was Paul saying that Aratus was inspired by God as well? Is every contemporary religious teacher inspired by God? No. The Bible is God's special, unique communication to humankind. God gave no other book in history to humankind. It is the written Word. In the same vein, no other prophets or teachers are inspired by God if they lead people away from faith in the Lord Jesus Christ. The Book of 1 John warns Christians to reject those who desire to draw us away from the biblical Christ.

Paul's point was that although Aratus's writings were not inspired by God, the poet's search for God was inspired by Him. God wants to have relationships with all people, and everyone yearns for that relationship.

Match Paul's arguments with their definitions to affirm Jesus' lordship.
___ **1. Creation**   **a. Jesus was the agent of creation.**
___ **2. Sovereignty**   **b. God inspires humanity's search for Him.**
___ **3. Universal need**   **c. God uses the details of our lives to bring us to Him.**

Day 4: Confining Jesus to One People

The third method that world religions and spiritualists use to reshape Jesus in their image is a type of religious racism. Some try to make Jesus a specific Messiah for only one specific group of people. The argument goes this way:

You say that Jesus is not just a prophet but Lord.
You say that Jesus is not a partner but Lord alone.
We respond that He is Lord to one specific group, in this case, the Jews.
All people have messiahs who come just to their group.

To this assumption Paul explicitly stated, " 'Having overlooked the times of ignorance, God now commands all people everywhere to repent' " (Acts 17:30). Paul left no room for negotiation. Christ's call to salvation extends to all peoples in all countries, from every tribe and every race.

Read 1 John 2:1-2 in the margin. Jesus is the propitiation for the sins of the _____ _____.

Read 2 Peter 3:9 in the margin. God is patient because He wants _____ to come to Him in repentance.

Explain That the Invitation Is Open

The world criticizes Christians for insisting that Jesus is the only way to be saved. Instead of being apologetic, emphasize God's miraculous, merciful provision of that one way. You have the opportunity to tell people: "Because of God's great love for you, He has provided a way for you to be forgiven of every sin you have committed, to escape punishment and death, and to enter His glorious presence for all eternity. That way is Jesus Christ." Although that way is exclusive, God's invitation is universal. Jesus is the way for everyone who comes to Him in faith.

Read Revelation 5:9 in the margin. Jesus' blood redeems people from every _____ and _____ and _____ and _____.

Christ came to earth, died on the cross, and rose in victory over death so that all people could be saved through faith in Him and live with Him forever. If His death had provided salvation for only one group of people, God would be unjust and arbitrary.

Mark the following statements *T* (true) or *F* (false).
___ **Jesus died to save everyone.**
___ **Jesus died only for the Jews.**
___ **Jesus is the only way to be saved.**
___ **God offers salvation to everyone who places faith in Christ.**
___ **God offers salvation only to Jews who come to Him in repentance.**

The following scriptural evidence supports the Christian conviction that Jesus Christ is the Lord of all people. Check your answers against these statements.
 • Sin came through one man named Adam (see Rom. 5:12-21).
 • Sin equally affected all men and women everywhere (see Rom. 5:12-21).
 • Jesus died for the sins of the whole world (see 1 John 2:1-2).
 • Christ is the only way to enter heaven (see John 14:6).
 • God wants everyone to repent (see 2 Pet. 3:9).
 • Every man and woman will someday face judgment (see Heb. 9:27).

"I am writing you these things so that you may not sin. But if anyone does sin, we have an advocate with the Father—Jesus Christ the righteous One. He Himself is the propitiation for our sins, and not only for ours, but also for those of the whole world."
1 John 2:1-2

"The Lord does not delay His promise, as some understand delay, but is patient with you, not wanting any to perish, but all to come to repentance."
2 Peter 3:9

"You [Jesus] are worthy to take the scroll and to open its seals; because You were slaughtered, and You redeemed people for God by Your blood from every tribe and language and people and nation."
Revelation 5:9

DEFINITION

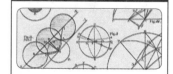

Propitiation

The truth that Jesus' action on the cross appeased or satisfied God, changing His wrath to favor toward humankind

- Every man and woman will be consigned to either heaven or hell (see Matt. 25:46).
- Christ is the sole criterion by which men and women will be judged (see Acts 17:31).
- God's plan is for people from every tribe, language, people, and nation to worship eternally around Christ's throne (see Rev. 5:9).

Jesus came not just to be Lord. He came to be Lord of all.

Day 5: Consigning Jesus to the Past

Skeptics and spiritualists make a last-ditch effort to relegate Jesus to a lower status than complete Lord. They argue that people needed faith and religion in a past time when we had neither the answers nor the capacity to resolve our problems for ourselves. We needed Jesus back then, they reason, because we needed to invent a superstition and a mythology to explain our deeper questions and longings. We have now evolved to a point that we no longer need Jesus, so the reasoning goes.

Humanity has now found the answers, discovered our origins, and proved our ability to govern our lives. Humans are at the center of this world, and the human mind is the conqueror.

How does Paul's address to the Athenians respond to this intellectual argument? Paul reminded the Athenians: " '[God] has set a day on which He is going to judge the world in righteousness by the Man He has appointed. He has provided proof of this to everyone by raising Him from the dead' " (Acts 17:31).

How do Paul's words refute the idea that Jesus must be consigned to the past?

_____

_____

In this one verse Paul gave several arguments that Jesus is Lord for all time. Not only will there be a reckoning, but God has also cemented that day in stone. The exact day of judgment is already determined.

Paul also preached that God will judge all people by the central and sole criterion of Jesus Christ. Literally, this verse means that He will judge in righteousness by the One He appointed. The criterion by which judgment will be measured has also been conspicuously chosen. We will not be judged by the standards of Muhammed, Vishnu, or Buddha. We will be judged by the model of Jesus.

Finally, Paul preached that God has the right to judge by this criterion because Jesus rose from the dead. This is the one central truth around which all others revolve. Jesus was resurrected. He rose from death to life. His resurrection defeated death, as Paul noted in 1 Corinthians 15:54-57: "Death has been swallowed up in victory. O Death, where is your victory? O Death, where is your sting? Now the sting of death is sin, and the power of sin is the law. But thanks be to God, who gives us the victory through our Lord Jesus Christ!"

The results of Paul's proclamation were mixed. Acts 17:32-34 notes: "When they heard about resurrection of the dead, some began to ridicule him. But others said, 'We will hear you about this again.' So Paul went out from their presence. However, some men joined him and believed, among whom were Dionysius the Areopagite, a woman named Damaris, and others with them."

Name the four ways our society tries to reshape Jesus.
• **By redefining Him as** _____
• **By realigning Him as** _____
• **By confining Him to one** _____
• **By consigning Him to the** _____

Should we become disheartened when people mock our allegiance to Christ as Lord, Lord alone, Lord of all, and Lord for all time? Of course not. Some of Paul's listeners were open to further discussion, while others accepted his message.

GLOBAL PERSPECTIVE

Would the Real Jesus Please Stand Up?

A television show's effort to discover the real Jesus was rooted in this guideline: "Every Christian sooner or later has to ask the question 'Who was Jesus really?'"

Public Broadcasting System's *Frontline* broadcast "From Jesus to Christ" reflected society's incomplete acceptance of Jesus. Acknowledging that "a number of different portraits of Jesus have emerged, certain issues dominate the emerging picture of the historical Jesus."

Among these are: (1) "The historical Jesus and the Jesus of the early church bear little resemblance to one another." The show argued that there is even less connection between the real Jesus and the Jesus of contemporary Christianity. In other words, we worship a made-up Jesus, not the Son of God who lived, died, and arose in the first century. (2) Jesus might or might not have seen Himself as the Messiah, "but he almost certainly did not see himself as divine." The implication is that if Jesus did not see Himself as divine, neither should His followers.

Society accepts Jesus, but what it accepts about Him may vary considerably. Few deny His existence in history. They just do not accept Him as Lord.[4]

Read 1 Corinthians 15:58 in the margin. How should we respond when we are ridiculed for speaking about Jesus?
○ **Argue**   ○ **Retaliate**   ○ **Keep working**   ○ **Give up**

"Be steadfast, immovable, always abounding in the Lord's work, knowing that your labor in the Lord is not in vain."

1 Corinthians 15:58

WITNESSING TIP

Show That God Reveals the Truth

Those who relegate Jesus to the past often believe that reason and science are capable of meeting human needs today. As a Christian, you can acknowledge the legitimacy of human discovery through valid forms of scientific research. However, because of our finite, sinful natures, humans are not capable of understanding all things, especially those of a spiritual nature. Explain that truth cannot be discovered but must be revealed. Point out the ways God has made Himself known to us, not only through nature (see Rom. 1:18-32) but also through His written Word (see 2 Tim. 3:15-17; 2 Pet. 1:19-21) and through His Son, Jesus Christ (see Phil. 2:6-10; Col. 2:9; Heb. 1:1-2).

Paul's words to the Corinthian church come in the context of Jesus' resurrection. In light of Jesus' victory over death, keep working to proclaim that He is Lord for all time.

The rest of this study will equip you to do just that. During the first three weeks of our study we overviewed cultural philosophies that are prevalent today, identified needs that people have, and established the unique beliefs that constitute a Christian worldview. Over the next four weeks we will use the worldview questions we studied in day 1 of this week to examine the beliefs of Hinduism, Buddhism, Judaism, and Islam. We will explore specific Christian responses to these beliefs and will identify ways to reach out and witness to followers of these faiths.

[1] "Americans Describe Their Views About Life After Death," *The Barna Update* [online], 21 October 2003 [cited 24 May 2005]. Available from the Internet: *www.barna.org.*

[2] Adelaide Midkiff, "Religious Fanatics Have Sanctioned Atrocities," *Tennessean* [online], 22 April 2005 [cited 3 May 2005]. Available from the Internet: *www.tennessean.com/opinion/letters/archives.*

[3] Paul Naras, "New Age: Defining the New Age," *The Global Oneness Commitment: Co-creating a Happy World* [cited 26 April 2005]. Available from the Internet: *www.experiencefestival.com/a/NewAge/id/35306.*

[4] Claudia Tikkun Setzer, "Jesus' Many Faces: The Historical Jesus," *PBS* [online], 17 July 1995 [cited 2 May 2005]. Available from the Internet: *www.pbs.org/wgbh/pages/frontline/shows/religion/jesus/tikkun.html.*

Viewer Guide
Group Session 3

Review Segment: A Not-So-Brave New World

We are a culture driven by _____.
Christians are not a people driven by feeling but by _____.
Jesus is the _____, _____, and _____ of our faith.

Our culture wants to _____ Jesus as a prophet, _____ Him as
a partner, _____ Him to one people, or _____ Him to the past.
Any _____ of Jesus changes the One of whom we are speaking.

It offends some people to say that Jesus is _____ alone.

Some things are more important than the fear of offending.
_____ is hanging in the balance.

Teaching Segment: Hinduism: Atheism with 330 Million Gods

In Hinduism you can be _____ and _____ at the same moment.
Central tenant: _____
  • Reincarnation of _____
  • Reincarnation of _____
  • Reincarnation of _____
  • Reincarnation of _____

The cosmic search for _____ gives birth to manifestations of Hindu teachings.
Karma, good or bad, is _____. Good karma causes you to be _____
as a better being. The pursuit of good karma unites Hinduism.

Hinduism holds to 330 million gods, yet not one is _____.

The belief in reincarnation plays out in _____.

Grace is a _____ concept to the Hindu.
What they call karma, you and I know as the _____ _____.

Hinduism offers _____ yet _____. Everything is tied
together in cosmic energy.

Jesus is the God who died for you. You cannot have better karma than that.
The key is _____.

Hinduism

Atheism with 330 Million Gods

When these events were over, Paul resolved in the Spirit to pass through Macedonia and Achaia and go to Jerusalem. "After I've been there," he said, "I must see Rome as well!" So after sending two of those who assisted him, Timothy and Erastus, to Macedonia, he himself stayed in the province of Asia for a while.

During that time there was a major disturbance about the Way. For a person named Demetrius, a silversmith who made silver shrines of Artemis, provided a great deal of business for the craftsmen. When he had assembled them, as well as the workers engaged in this type of business, he said: "Men, you know that our prosperity is derived from this business. You both see and hear that not only in Ephesus, but in almost the whole province of Asia, this man Paul has persuaded and misled a considerable number of people by saying that gods made by hand are not gods! So not only do we run a risk that our business may be discredited, but also that the temple of the great goddess Artemis may be despised and her magnificence come to the verge of ruin—the very one whom the whole province of Asia and the world adore." When they had heard this, they were filled with rage and began to cry out, "Great is Artemis of the Ephesians!" Acts 19:21-28

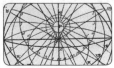

GLOBAL SNAPSHOT

- More than one billion people claim to follow Hinduism, but many actually follow folk versions that include ancestral and animal worship.
- Hinduism is strongest in India and Pakistan but grows most rapidly in the United States and western Europe.

THIS WEEK'S GOAL

No.4

After this week's study you will be able to—
- state basic Hindu beliefs;
- give a biblical response to each belief;
- suggest ways to witness to Hindus.

Stone Soup for the Soul

Even though it was my first debate, I was certain that I had won from the outset. A communications business was offering so-called diversity training and, as part of its comparative-religions emphasis, had asked me to speak, along with a Hindu priest from the local temple. After I had made my introduction, the priest stepped to the podium and began: "I must say for the purposes of honesty and disclosure that I also accept Jesus as God without hesitation. I believe Jesus is divine and was completely the revelation of the Lord."

Was the Hindu priest confessing Christ as Lord? Was he leaving Hinduism to claim Jesus as Prophet, Priest, and King? No, the Hindu was simply stating the central premise of Hinduism: a belief in the theological equivalent of stone soup.

Perhaps you remember the classic fable "Stone Soup." As a town descends into poverty and starvation, one person sets up a boiling cauldron of water in the city square. One by one, townspeople add the meager remnants of their pantries. Eventually, cooperation and generosity create an amazing soup, and the city eats. Hinduism operates much like the stone-soup metaphor because it is an amalgamation of many religions. It adds dashes of Christianity, Islam, Zoroastrianism, and other religions to one large pot of polytheism. The resulting dish is Hinduism. Consequently, as Hinduism enters a culture, it introduces ingredients from every religion to that culture.

An estimated 14 to 15 percent of the world's population claims to be Hindu. As you study this week, be forewarned that Hinduism is a confusing religion. Imagine that you were raised in a world of many conflicting gods, much like the first-century culture Paul confronted. Wouldn't you want to know something—anything—for sure?

Day 1: Who Am I? God and Humanity

In its more than four-thousand-year history, Hinduism has absorbed customs, doctrines, and concepts from virtually every source. Many of these beliefs may contradict the initial core of Hindu beliefs, but that is Hinduism's *modus operandi*. Because the nature of Hinduism is so complicated, every variation is simply viewed as another stream to the river. There are Hindus who believe in no gods, Hindus who believe in one god, and Hindus who believe in many gods!

Is it possible to understand such a complex religion? We can start by identifying the variations of Hinduism and the gods Hindus serve.

Vedic Hinduism

The term *Hinduism* comes from the Indus River that flows through present-day Pakistan. Four thousand years ago the region was the home of the Dravidians, a dark-skinned and highly superstitious people. Scholars believe they held to a form of natural and sexual worship, mixing a desire for abundant harvests and personal fertility. Around 2000 B.C. the Aryans conquered the Dravidians, bringing their lighter-skinned warriors over the Caucasus Mountains. The Aryans, a polytheistic group (believing in many gods), incorporated the Dravidian gods into their form or religion. The Aryan hymns and doctrines were collected in four books:

1. Vedas
2. Brahmanas
3. Aranyakas
4. Upanishads

These four books are considered sacred to Vedic Hindus, containing the central belief of their system: pantheism. This system holds that a god did not create the world; God is the world. According to the Vedic system, we are all part of God, and this God is part of everything. God is not necessarily a personal, intimate, or even intelligent god. God is Brahma, the impersonal highest being.

In this belief system, God is somewhat like a molecular fingerprint. Wherever there is life, this "God stuff" is in it. Because all living things, including humans, are part of God, they are divine. Therefore, the basic problem for humankind is not sin but ignorance of our divinity.

Underline the correct word(s) in each pair to identify Hindu beliefs.
In Hinduism God is (a personal being, an impersonal force).
   God (created, is) the world.
   Humans are (part of, separate from) God.
   Humans are (mortal, divine).
   Humanity's basic problem is (sin, ignorance).

Because God is part of everything, the various forms of nature are godlike. For example, the god of the atmosphere is Indra, and the god of fire is Agni. These smaller gods, called demigods, all share the same essence of the god Brahma. The priests of this system, known as Brahmins, are part of the highest social level in Hindu countries.

Upanishadic Hinduism

Around 600 B.C. another sect of Hinduism formed, known as Upanishad. It also held to a belief in Brahma but was much more pessimistic. For the Upanishads, life is depressing, and the only way out is to be reborn countless times. This belief is the core of reincarnation. This transmigration from one being to another, known as *samsara*, comes when we become better, kinder, and more spiritual. If we achieve the ultimate spirituality through chanting and meditation, we can become part of Brahma.

By the Upanishadic period Hinduism developed a belief in three specific forms of Brahma, somewhat like a trinity:
   Brahma is the creator.
   Vishnu is the preserver.
   Shiva is the destroyer.

DEFINITION

Polytheism
A belief in many gods

Pantheism
The belief that everything is God or a part of God

Explain the concept of reincarnation in your own words. _____

_____

Vishnu Hinduism

Another very popular form of Hinduism is called Vishnu. The Vishnuites worship the specific god Vishnu, who they believe has come to earth nine times as an *avatar* (savior) to rescue humanity. Vishnu has already come to earth as a fish, a turtle, a boar, a half-lion and half-man, a dwarf, Parasurama, Rama, Krishna, and Buddha. Rama and Krishna are considered the most important of these incarnations. Vishnu Hindus await the coming of Kalki, the final rescuer.

Shivaite Hinduism

The most violent form of Hinduism is the sect that worships the destroyer god Shiva. Adherents also worship his wife, who goes by various names—Kali, Sati, Deva, and others. This form of Hinduism, known to be bloody and immoral, is responsible for much of the bloodshed in present-day India.

Populist Hinduism

A cultic form of Hinduism exists among the more than one billion inhabitants of India. The people borrow gods from the various Hindu systems but also add ancestral worship. This practice may be confusing to Christians, who look for clear categories and denominations. In the Asiatic regions of the world where Hinduism is strong, temples rise up everywhere, many of which are unaffiliated with any branch of Hinduism. Spiritual teachers (*gurus*) and holy men (*swamis*) wander the continent and attract followers in the thousands. This form of Hinduism, the most polytheistic, can cause much frustration for Christians. When evangelists come to a city and call for the people to repent and believe in Jesus, Hindus walk forward in masses.

Why would this response by Hindus be a problem? _____

_____

Because Hindus accept multiple gods, they may not be accepting Jesus as their only Savior and Lord. They might simply be adding Him to their collection of gods!

Western Hinduism

Beginning with Ralph Waldo Emerson and Henry David Thoreau in the 19th century, the West has gradually assimilated Hinduism into our culture. Aldous Huxley, the author of *Brave New World,* became an ardent follower of Hinduism. Mohandas Gandhi popularized the Hindu system of pacifism. In the 1960s the Beatles embraced a Western form of Hinduism known as Transcendental Meditation.

DEFINITION

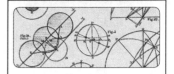

Reincarnation

The belief that the souls of the dead successively return to earth in new bodies or forms

One with the Divine

Hindu influences are everywhere in our culture. Environmentalists espouse a belief in the common energy we share with trees and animals. Angel worshipers seek contact with angels as minigods or spiritual guides. Even the use of the horoscope has a Hindu flavor, because an astrologer believes that instead of acting by choice, we are compelled to act by the forces and energies of the universe, such as aligning planets. Someone who relies on a horoscope says, "Of course I'm afraid of commitment: I'm a Scorpio."

Hinduism has also launched eco-Hinduism in the West. Activists argue that because God is in everything, they must embrace vegetarianism and ecological preservation. They find purpose in opposing hunting, the growth of business, and war. Hinduism serves as the great unifier in many social-protest movements today.

Check the Hindu influences you have observed in society.
○ **Pacifism**
○ **Environmental activism**
○ **Horoscope**
○ **Angel worship**
○ **Belief in reincarnation**
○ **Belief in pantheism**

Confronting the Truth

In contrast to the impersonal god Brahma, the God of the Bible is personal and knowable. He talks, rebukes, feels, becomes angry, is jealous, laughs, loves, and has a personal name (see Gen. 1:29-30; 6:6; Ex. 3:14-15; 20:5; Lev. 20:23; Ps. 2:4; 59:9; Zeph. 3:17). The Bible clearly rejects a belief in pantheism. Although God created the universe, He is distinct and separate from His creation (see Rom. 1:22-23).

Christians must also challenge the Hindu view of humanity. The basic human problem is not ignorance of divinity but sin—willful rebellion against God and His commandments (see Rom. 1:28-32; 2:1-16; 3:23; Gal. 3:22; 1 John 1:8-10). Although God created people in His image (see Gen. 1:27), we inherit a sinful nature and choose to sin against Him (see Rom. 3:23; 5:12). The Bible does not teach that we are part of God; we can pray to God but can never become God. Share with Hindus that they can become acceptable to Him only by repenting of their sin and accepting the atoning work of Jesus Christ (see Rom. 3:24-26).

Match the Hindu belief with the correct Christian response.

___ 1. God is impersonal.   a. God is distinct from His creation.

___ 2. Pantheism: everything is God.   b. God is personal and knowable.

___ 3. Humanity is divine.   c. Humanity's problem is sin.

___ 4. Humanity's problem is ignorance.   d. Humans are distinct from God.

Return again to the scenario in today's Scripture. Having heard of Paul's message in Ephesus and elsewhere that there is only one God, Demetrius was in a panic. As a silversmith, he had a vested interest in the many gods people worshiped. Because Paul preached that Jesus Christ alone is Savior, he posed a threat to Demetrius's livelihood. Demetrius gathered the idol makers and sought a resolution to the problem. Paul was costing them money, and they were ready to stop him.

Demetrius unwittingly got the message right! Paul was in fact saying that the idols made with men's hands were no gods at all. In the middle of a polytheistic world, Jesus was not to be confused with the pantheon of gods.

How clear is your witness that Christ alone is Savior? How would you respond?
○ **If someone says "god," I suppose he or she means the one true God.**
○ **I figure if someone is religious, that's good enough.**
○ **I work to clearly understand what others believe and to explain Jesus Christ.**
○ **This all just seems hopelessly complicated to me.**

The time has passed when most Americans shared a common worldview. For the sake of eternity, we must be clear in our faith and witness. We have to work to help people understand that the God of the Bible is the only God. Everything else is idolatry.

Day 2: How Can I Know? Authority and Truth

Today we will examine six concepts that form the nucleus of Hinduism. Regardless of the sect, each Hindu adheres to some form of these principles.

Brahma: Reality

The ultimate reality or god of Hinduism is Brahma. Even the atheistic systems of Hinduism believe in the ultimate goal known as Brahma. As one of the sacred texts of the Upanishads (Taittiriya) states, "Brahma is he whom speech cannot express, and from whom the mind ... comes away baffled." Hindus consider Brahma an *it* rather than a *he*. Hindus believe that the human soul, known as the *atman*, connects to Brahma. A Hindu's ultimate hope is that his *atman* unites with Brahma.

Maya: Illusion

The word *maya* is loosely translated *illusion*. Existence and reality, for the Hindu, are not necessarily absolute. For instance, if I asked whether your dreams are real, your answer would be both yes and no. Yes, the dream is real inasmuch as you experienced it, but no, it did not actually take place. You may have felt that you were running from a monster in your dream, but you were in fact soundly asleep in your bed.

Hinduism teaches that all suffering is simply an illusion. It is not real. Like the cult Christian Science centuries later, Hinduism denies the actual substance of suffering. It is *maya*—an illusion.

Moksha: Salvation

Although the word *moksha* (also *mukti*) is translated *liberation*, we can best understand it as salvation. *Moksha* is a process by which people are freed from the cycle of reincarnation and suffering. In this way Hindus believe humanity can be released from the bondage of life.

Samsara: Reincarnation

Hindus believe in a continuous chain of reward and punishment called reincarnation. If someone attains enlightenment and goodness, the result is freedom from the cycle (*moksha*). However, if a person is unable to become good or maintains evil, they will be reincarnated based on the level of evil. Reincarnation applies not only to life (you come back as a frog, for example) but also to social structures, known as castes. If you are better than you were in a past life, you advance upward in the social caste.

Karma: The Law of Moral Consequence

Karma is the guiding force behind Hinduism. The word actually means *action*, but the concept is simple: payback. It is the law of consequence. You are recompensed based on your actions, and when you perform a righteous act, you receive a reward.

Conversely, when you commit evil, you receive evil in return, and this is your karma as well. Karma can be received in this life or in a later existence, but it cannot be changed once it is determined. Hindus believe in ultimate payback.

WITNESSING TIP

Build on Respect for the Word

Hindus respect sacred writings. Many Hindus will attentively listen to an explanation of the teachings of the Bible. Use this openness to present biblical truth about God, Jesus, and salvation. Don't allow yourself to get lost in the maze of Hindu complexity. Present the clear witness of Scripture to the basic beliefs you have studied in today's lesson.

Bhakti: Devotion to a Personal God

One of the latest additions to the sacred books of Hinduism is also the most famous. The Bhagavad Gita, written during the first century, enunciates the concept of *bhakti*, devotion to a personal god. The book consists of a long poem that is a conversation between Krishna and the warrior Arjuna. The warrior is torn between loving his own relatives and his duty to kill them in battle. "If I am faithful," he reasons, "I will kill my relatives, but I will suffer. What should I do?" In the end Arjuna abandons his own will and devotes himself to Vishnu. He suffers and kills his family but finds salvation through obedience.

The concept of *bhakti* has fueled much of the warfare in Hinduism. The reasoning goes this way: "If I want to achieve good karma, I will be devoted to my god at all costs. This devotion may bring suffering, but I must do it to bring release. Besides, suffering is an illusion anyway (*maya*)."

Mark each of the following true (*T*) or false (*F*) to clarify your understanding of Hindu beliefs.

___ 1. Brahma is a personal, transcendent god who exists apart from creation.

___ 2. *Maya* means that all suffering is merely an illusion.

___ 3. Reincarnation is a cycle of reward and punishment that can be escaped only through enlightenment and goodness.

___ 4. Salvation for Hinduism means escape from the cycle of reincarnation and suffering.

___ 5. Karma is very similar to the Christian concept of sin.

___ 6. The concept of devotion to a personal god has fueled much of the violence in Hinduism.

All of the statements except 1 and 5 are true.

Confronting the Truth

Each system of Hinduism attempts to resolve the enormous issues of suffering, sin, and guilt. Though the answers Hindus offer are eternally incorrect, they give us clear points at which we can engage Hindus in discussion and present the gospel.

Read each Scripture in the margin, matching the reference with the correct teaching. Each Scripture speaks to a specific Hindu belief.

___ 1. Romans 12:19	a. Christ suffered for sin.
___ 2. Hebrews 9:27	b. People die once and are then judged.
___ 3. 1 Peter 2:24	c. Christ purchased salvation for us on the cross.
___ 4. 1 Peter 3:18	d. Vengeance belongs to God.

- The law of karma, or cause and effect, is refuted by God's claim of sovereignty over vengeance (see Rom. 12:19). God's merciful provision for the forgiveness of sin eliminates the need for humans to live by the law of karma.
- Christ bore suffering on the cross (see 1 Pet. 3:18). Our greatest need is not escape from suffering but deliverance from sin.
- Hebrews 9:27 repudiates any concept of reincarnation. Christ's atonement provides the way for people to receive forgiveness for their sin once and for all.
- Salvation is found in the One who died for us (see 1 Pet. 2:24). Christ, the Lamb of God, offers the answer for Hindus who are trying to earn salvation through the cycle of reincarnation. He suffered. He died. He rose from the dead. He is our advocate. He is our hope. He is our salvation.

The Bible refutes all Hindu doctrine. In it believers have a truly reliable source of authority that shows the only way to God.

"It is written: Vengeance belongs to Me; I will repay, says the Lord."
Romans 12:19

"It is appointed for people to die once—and after this, judgment."
Hebrews 9:27

"He Himself bore our sins in His body on the tree, so that, having died to sins, we might live for righteousness; by His wounding you have been healed."
1 Peter 2:24

"Christ also suffered for sins once for all, the righteous for the unrighteous, that He might bring you to God, after being put to death in the fleshly realm but made alive in the spiritual realm."
1 Peter 3:18

Day 3: Why Am I Here? Purpose and Ethics

Does Hindu existence have a purpose? Does a Hindu operate by a cohesive ethical standard? These questions seem simplistic, but the Hindu concept of life itself makes these questions relevant. Remember, in Hinduism all forms of life—trees, plants, animals, and humans—share a common existence together. A strong corporate, I'm-just-a-cog-in-the-wheel mentality exists in Hinduism. A Hindu could reasonably ask, "If I am just a part of a greater god, do I really matter?"

A Hindu is also limited by his caste. He lives within the parameters of his station in life, and his greatest hope is to be reincarnated at a higher level. The caste system (called *varna*) is unique to Hinduism. In the Hindu caste and social structure, you are born in your caste. You live and work in your caste. You relate only to those in your caste. You marry in your caste. You will die in your caste. Do not fight it. Accept it.

According to Hinduism, Brahma created the first man, named Manu. Out of Manu came four separate and distinct types of people:

Brahmins came from Manu's head. The highest caste of people, they serve as the priests of Hinduism.

Kshatriyas came from Manu's hands. They are the rulers, politicians, and warriors. They compose the ruling class of kings and senators, along with soldiers, who hold an exalted position in Hinduism.

Vaisyas came from Manu's thighs. They are the creative caste of craftsmen and farmers. Think of them as the businessmen and store owners who keep the economy alive with their entrepreneurial spirit and creativity.

Shudras came from Manu's feet. These are manual laborers and the servants.
As the caste system developed in history, each category also subdivided, so today there are more than three thousand distinct levels of social status.

One final caste must be mentioned. The **Harijan,** also known as Outcastes or Untouchables, make up a large portion of the Hindu population. In Hindu history the Untouchables were considered almost subhuman, the lowest form of Hindu existence. Today they are given the worst jobs and occupy the lowest stations in life. The other Hindus hold Outcastes in almost visceral contempt and scorn. Along with the Shudras, they are not allowed to read the Vedas. Outcastes drink polluted water, eat contaminated meat, and die from starvation and disease.

Ethically, Hinduism is a difficult system to embrace. When India became a nation in 1947, the brutalization of the Untouchables was deemed illegal, but the caste system continues to this

WITNESSING TIP

Share God's Love

Your attitude when relating to Hindus oppressed by caste and karma must be one of love. God accepts and loves each Hindu, and we can open the door to a Christian witness by showing that love. As a relationship develops, you may be able to share that Christ loves every person, regardless of social or economic position (see Luke 15: 19:1-10; John 3:16; 1 John 4:9-10).

day. Most Hindus believe that karma is extended only within their own caste, and they don't believe that subjugating lower castes hurts their status.

Check the responses that accurately describe a Hindu's purpose and ethics.
○ **A Hindu's highest hope is reincarnation to a higher level.**
○ **The caste system limits both the Hindu's hopes and compassion.**
○ **Karma leads people to fight for justice for all members of society.**
○ **Suffering must be relieved because it is an illusion.**

The combination of fatalism and illusion (*maya*) creates an abysmal existence for the majority of Hindus. They suffer horribly, but suffering is considered an illusion. Therefore, a Hindu feels compelled to do good works to receive good karma and avoid evil deeds to achieve liberation.

Confronting the Truth
In Acts 19 the craftsmen's accusation against Paul was clear: he was claiming that God is the only God. However, Paul did not preach a racist gospel—that God was the God of only Jews or Christians. The accounts of the second and third missionary journeys show that Paul presented salvation in Christ to both the rich and the poor. According to Acts 19:21, Paul was willing to go anywhere to share Christ.

The truth that Christ offers salvation to all people is vitally important when presenting Jesus to a belief system saturated in caste. Jesus ministered to both the rich man and the impoverished woman at the well (see John 4). He reached beyond the confines of castes and saw the heart.

In addition, Jesus did not deal with crowds but with individuals. He viewed each person with value and purpose. This approach is vital in presenting Christ to a Hindu. Jesus said that God has even counted the hairs on each person's head (see Matt. 10:30). This was a statement not only of God's sovereignty but also of His intimacy.

Review the two previous paragraphs and name two ways Christianity offers hope for the fatalism of the caste system.

1. _____

2. _____

You have the opportunity to share with Hindus that Christ offers salvation for all people, not just those in certain castes. He also cares about and pursues a relationship with each individual.

Day 4: Where Am I Going? Eternity and Legacy

When Paul proclaimed the one true God in Ephesus, he declared that the city's many idols were not gods. Demetrius, the silversmith, marshaled opposition against Paul by saying to the craftsmen of the city: " 'Not only do we run a risk that our business may be discredited, but also that the temple of the great goddess Artemis may be despised and her magnificence come to the verge of ruin—the very one whom the whole province of Asia and the world adore.' " When they had heard this, they were filled with rage and began to cry out, " 'Great is Artemis of the Ephesians!' " (Acts 19:27-28).

Why are we using this text to discuss Hinduism? Was the temple of Artemis (Diana) dedicated to Hinduism? No, but Diana is a symbol of and an analogy for the Hindu concepts of nature and life. The temple of Diana in Ephesus had taken more than two hundred years to build. At 425 feet long and 220 feet wide, the structure was virtually unmatched in human achievement. It was surrounded by 127 columns, each 60 feet high. Imagine a temple almost as wide and long as a football field. Diana was always depicted as the mother of all creation, covered with breasts with which she would nurse all living creatures. Statues of this goddess often depicted her legs covered with the heads of animals, suggesting a symbiosis of humans and beasts.

Like the mythology of Diana, Hinduism has an almost evolutionary outlook on life. The Hindu concepts of works, reincarnation, and salvation are all tied together in one sweeping system of recycling. Hindus believe that if we commit evil acts rather than good ones, we can be reincarnated as an animal or even worse. Works and motivations are seen as pregnant with repercussions (karma). Hindus believe that we are all part of a cosmic wheel of destiny.

Write a summary statement beside each key Hindu principle below. Review day 2 if needed to refresh your memory.

Brahma: _____

Maya: _____

Moksha: _____

Samsara: _____

Karma: _____

Bhakti: _____

Contradictions abound in Hinduism. Although a person's destiny can be cursed to a lower state as an animal, some animals are considered sacred. Reverence for the cow appears to contradict reincarnation. These verses from the Atharva Veda illustrate the Hindu belief that the cow holds an almost godlike position in Hinduism:

> *Worship, O Cow, to thy tail-hair, and to thy hooves and to thy form! Hither-*
> *ward we invite with prayer the Cow who pours a thousand streams, by*
> *Whom the heaven, By whom the earth, by whom these waters are preserved.*
> *... They call the Cow immortal life, pay homage to the Cow as Death. She*
> *hath become this universe ... hath become the Gods, and men, and Spirits. ...*
> *The Cow is Heaven, the Cow is Earth, the Cow is Vishnu, Lord of Life*
> *(Atharva Veda, X:10).*

How is this possible? Some Hindus believe that the cow contains the spirits of dead ancestors. Yet they do not view their ancestors as having gone lower but higher in the reincarnation cycle.

Confronting the Truth

Christians believe that God is the Author of everything and that all the world is His magnificent creation. But in contrast to Hindu belief, we must distinguish God's children from the rest of His creation. God created three kinds of life: unconscious life—plants; conscious life—animals; and self-conscious life—humans.

Plants are living objects that operate by cycles of birth, nourishment, growth, and death. Animals display emotions; yet they function only by instinct. An animal cannot question a decision or appreciate the beauty of a sunset. Only human beings have spirits. Only humans, created and shaped by the hand of God, are self-conscious. They doubt and question because they have the capacity to choose between right and wrong, devotion and duty.

Read the following Scriptures in your Bible. Then match the references with the summary statements.

___ **1. Exodus 12:8**   **a. God declared all animals ceremonially clean to eat.**

___ **2. Deuteronomy 12:26-28**   **b. God commanded the Israelites to eat the Passover lamb.**

___ **3. Acts 11:4-9**   **c. God permitted eating the sacrifice offering.**

The Bible does not prohibit eating meat. The first bloodshed in the animal kingdom took place by God's hand. After Adam and Eve sinned, God made clothing for them—"clothing out of skins" (Gen. 3:21). Further, Old Testament Scripture encouraged eating the meat of sacrificial offerings not only by the priests but also by the people (see Ex. 12:8; Deut. 12:26-28). In Acts 11:4-9 God declared all animals ceremonially clean to eat.

Although people have dominion over creation (see Gen. 2:19), we are not free to abuse it. God holds us accountable for our stewardship of the resources He has given us. Our witness to Hindus is enhanced by a reasonable respect for God's creation.

The Hindu concept of reincarnation denies Christ's sacrifice on the cross and His shedding of blood as atonement for sin.

Which response best summarizes the teaching of Hebrews 9:27-28 in the margin?
- ○ **We die once and face judgment based on Christ's sacrifice to take away sin.**
- ○ **We die many times in a cyclical effort to replace bad karma with good.**

> **WITNESSING TIP**
>
> ## Help the Hindu Break Free
>
> As a Christian, you have good news for Hindus trapped by a belief in reincarnation. Christ's triumph over sin means that Hindus who accept Christ can break free of that cycle. Share with the Hindu Christ's triumph over sin and His taking on Himself the penalty of humankind's sin (see Mark 10:32-45; John 8:1-11; Rom. 8:1-17). Through Christ they can be free from the guilt that results from their actions. They don't have to carry out works intended to bring salvation. Christ's forgiveness cleanses them from sin.

"Just as it is appointed for people to die once—and after this, judgment—so also the Messiah, having been offered once to bear the sins of many, will appear a second time, not to bear sin, but to bring salvation to those who are waiting for Him."
Hebrews 9:27-28

Jesus addressed the solemn severity of eternal reward and punishment in a parable that cuts to the heart of Hindu doctrine. In Luke 12:16-21 He emphasized our personal responsibility for our earthly life: " 'A rich man's land was very productive. He thought to himself, "What should I do, since I don't have anywhere to store my crops? I will do this," he said. "I'll tear down my barns and build bigger ones and store all my grain and my goods there." Then I'll say to myself, "You have many goods stored up for many years. Take it easy; eat, drink, and enjoy yourself." But God said to him, "You fool! This very night your life is demanded of you. And the things you have prepared—whose will they be?" That's how it is with the one who stores up treasure for himself and is not rich toward God.' "

Recall the six degrees of separation from week 1. Which of the six gives hope to the dismal system of reincarnation and karma?

_____

How does Christ's sacrifice on the cross offer a better answer to sin than reincarnation?

_____

By receiving forgiveness of sin through faith in Christ, Hindus can be free of the burden of trying to earn salvation in their earthly lives and can live in the confidence of eternal life that Jesus promises.

Day 5: Is There Any Hope? Salvation and Security

Hindus seek to attain salvation (*moksha*) through one of three methods. All three entirely depend on the individual; therefore, all three deny Christ's substitutionary atonement. As you read these methods, ask God to help you sense the Hindu's depth of despair. Notice the excruciating lengths to which Hindus are willing to go to find a sense of peace (*nirvana*) and assurance.

It is the same desperation Paul witnessed in Ephesus. When Demetrius's fellow idol makers perceived the threat to their belief system, "they were filled with rage and began to cry out, 'Great is Artemis of the Ephesians!'" (Acts 19:28). Similarly, instead of recognizing the futility of their system of salvation, Hindus intensify their efforts and works. They shout for their gods and yet cannot drown out the cry of Calvary: " 'It is finished!' " (John 19:30).

CULTURE CLASH

Reincarnation

The Hindu teaching of reincarnation has infected American culture. How many times have you heard statements like the following?

"In the next life that person will suffer."

"In my next life I hope to come back as a ..."

"In a past life I believe I must have been a ..."

Evangelical Christians often embrace Hindu concepts unwittingly. Some believe in ghosts as the spirits of departed loved ones who had unresolved issues. Others embrace a vegetarian lifestyle as an outgrowth of a spiritual union with the animal kingdom.

The Way of Works: Karma Yoga

Through rituals, ceremonies, and acts of self-denial, Hindus believe they can gain salvation. Life on earth is considered a training ground for the soul. Therefore, they go to great lengths to purify their thoughts and deeds, often by excruciating methods. Some Hindus have been known to stand for years at a time, sleeping by leaning against a board, to reach a level of holiness. They embark on long pilgrimages to sacred sites, traveling without money, to prove their devotion. They fast for prolonged periods of time. They keep silence for years and even decades to prove their worth and achieve good karma.

Are the acts described above—
○ **self-sacrificing acts of love to serve others?**
○ **God-honoring acts to glorify Him?**
○ **self-centered efforts to relieve personal suffering?**

Talismans, spells, and even demonic incantations are all included in Hindu worship. Street vendors often sell charms that ward off bad karma and invite good karma. Thousands of rituals are believed to promote salvation, and specific sects or forms of Hinduism recommend particular rituals. Ultimately, because all forms of works salvation are self-centered, they are self-defeating.

The Way of Knowledge: Jnana Marga

The second method of salvation in Hinduism involves knowledge. Because ignorance is seen as the reason for suffering and pain, spiritual knowledge is viewed as a direct path of salvation. The greatest mental error in Hinduism is the ignorance of humanity's union with Brahma. Through various forms of meditation, recitation, and study, Hindu students gain intellectual enlightenment or spiritual intuition that brings a realization of oneness with Brahma and therefore salvation.

Ignorance in the Hindu system means—
○ **lack of knowledge about God;**
○ **failure to realize your own divinity;**
○ **failure to love God and love your neighbor.**

Many times knowledge is found at the feet of wise teachers, who often establish teaching centers in remote locations. These gurus or swamis demand absolute obedience to their teachings. Students are first shown the error of their previous knowledge, and only after their suppositions have been destroyed can they be properly trained. This process, which frequently takes years, requires strict discipline.

The Way of Devotion: Bhakti Marga

The final method of *moksha* combines the first two. Hindus who seek true knowledge and practice good works are on the pathway of devotion, known as the *bhakti marga*. This devotion is the worship Hindus offer to the god or gods they recognize. The path of devotion involves intricate rituals, known as yoga, that are designed to demonstrate worshipers' sincerity. These rituals include meditation (*raja* yoga), chanting, and a desire to lose themselves in Brahma. For endless hours Hindu worshipers are commanded to concentrate on one word or phrase (mantra) that serves to release their minds from worry or thought. These acts of devotion are all intended to bring participants into a state of unconscious transcendence. In this state they become almost immobile, and their minds are almost catatonic.

Confronting the Truth

If anyone could be saved by works, Hindus would certainly be at the top of the list. The agonizing lengths to which Hindus will go to achieve peace are almost unbearable. Many elderly Hindus have literally dedicated years to agonizing acts, such as lying on a bed of nails, to prove themselves worthy of a higher reincarnation.

However, the entire system is futile. Regardless of the devotion, Hindus never achieve any certainty. Instead, the admission of peace is seen as a step backward. True piety is characterized by anguish or at the very least the lack of comfort. Furthermore, the caste system inherent in Hinduism dooms the individual to a limited hope. Hindus can only dream of reaching a higher level of consciousness, and depending on where they start, the goal is not salvation but just a small step upward.

Read the Scriptures in the margin. Then write on the chart the ways the Scriptures answer the Hindu beliefs.

Hindu Belief	Biblical Truth
Brahma is an impersonal force.	Matthew 6:9
Hinduism denies a sin nature and evil.	Psalm 51:4; Romans 3:23
Hinduism ties salvation to works.	1 John 2:2
Hinduism offers countless second chances.	Hebrews 9:27

The entire Hindu system denies biblical Christianity. Brahma is an impersonal force, while the God of the Bible is described as Father. Hinduism denies a sin nature and even denies evil itself. Yet the Bible clearly teaches that we sin against a righteous God to whom we are accountable (see Ps. 51:4). Hinduism inextricably ties salvation to works, while the Bible offers Christ's sacrifice as our redemption. Hinduism offers countless second chances, but the Bible teaches that we are given one life on earth, followed by a judgment.

A Christian witness again centers on Paul's notorious proclamation: the resurrection. As Paul confronted the Greek world, he placed the entire weight of the Christian witness on

WITNESSING TIP

Offer Hope for Peace

The Hindu quest for peace and bliss can be met only in Christ, the author and giver of peace, with the promise of heavenly blessings and eternal fellowship with God (see John 6:35-40; 14:1-7; Rom. 5:1-11). Explain that Jesus broke the power of death and that believers go to be with Him when they die. Eternal hope lies not in an impersonal absorption into God but in a conscious existence and personal fellowship with God forever (see Matt. 22:32; 2 Cor. 5:8; Phil. 1:23).

"Our Father in heaven, Your name be honored as holy."
Matthew 6:9

"Against You—You alone— I have sinned and done this evil in Your sight."
Psalm 51:4

"All have sinned and fall short of the glory of God."
Romans 3:23

"He Himself [Jesus] is the propitiation for our sins, and not only for ours, but also for those of the whole world."
1 John 2:2

"It is appointed for people to die once—and after this, judgment."
Hebrews 9:27

Christ's resurrection. If Christ conquered the grave, as He did, His promise was sure, and we are forgiven. If Christ arose on the third day, then His death was proved and His sacrifice certain. Christ shed His blood as the sacrificial Lamb, thus providing salvation for us. Salvation is a gift from God through faith in Jesus (see Eph. 2:8-9).

It is impossible to earn salvation by good works. In the same way, religious deeds and exercises do not provide salvation (see Matt. 7:22-23; Rom. 9:32; Gal. 2:16). Hindus' exertion results only in further exertion. Pain denied begets further pain.

Perhaps Paul had just this type of belief system in mind when he wrote Titus 3:3-8. Read these verses in the margin with fresh eyes and grateful hearts. The futility of such belief systems is apparent (see v. 3), but the grace and mercy we have received show up in dramatic contrast (see vv. 4-7). And the good deeds follow (see v. 8).

Read the witnessing tip on page 81. How has God brought peace in your life? Thoughtfully write how you would testify to a Hindu about God's peace.

"We too were once foolish, disobedient, deceived, captives of various passions and pleasures, living in malice and envy, hateful, detesting one another. But when the goodness and love for man appeared from God our Savior, He saved us—not by works of righteousness that we had done, but according to His mercy, through the washing of regeneration and renewal by the Holy Spirit. This Spirit He poured out on us abundantly through Jesus Christ our Savior, so that having been justified by His grace, we may become heirs with the hope of eternal life. This saying is trustworthy. I want you to insist on these things, so that those who have believed God might be careful to devote themselves to good works. These are good and profitable for everyone."
Titus 3:3-8

A Comparison of Beliefs

	Christianity	Hinduism
God	One God. Personal and knowable. Distinct from creation.	Impersonal and unknowable.
Jesus	Unique Son of God who provided salvation through atoning death and resurrection.	An enlightened man.
Source of Authority	Bible is divinely inspired and preserved and contains perfect instruction and truth.	The Vedas and other writings.
Humanity	Not part of God. Sinful by nature.	Divine. Part of God. Basically good.
Sin	Sinful nature and choices are humanity's problem.	No sin. Ignorance of divinity is humanity's problem.
Salvation	Accepting God's gift of forgiveness through faith in Jesus Christ.	Escaping law of karma and becoming one with God.

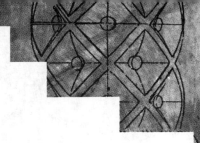

Viewer Guide
Group Session 4

Review Segment: Hinduism

In the Hindu world everything is _____.

In Hinduism time is _____ and _____. Cyclical time for the Hindi is _____.
Good karma leads to _____ or paradise.

For the Christian, time is _____. In eternity we won't measure time in 24-hour increments.

These borrow from concepts of the Hindu spirit realm:
- Tarot cards
- Astrology
- Psychics
- Crystal readers
- Horoscopes

There is only one _____, three persons. God became man in Jesus Christ so that men could _____ with God, not become _____.

Teaching Segment: Buddhism: The Old New Age

In Buddhism we all have the same _____: the mother earth.

In Buddhism, if there is no god but mother earth and everybody is an enlightened being, suffering is _____.

The only place of healing is a place of _____.

As Buddhists alleviate suffering, they find the one thing they seek: _____.

Some people confuse Buddhism and New Age teaching with _____.
- Humanism puts man at the center of all truth and knowledge.
- Buddhism/New Age = naturalism; the mother earth is the source of energy and healing.

Buddhists avoid talking about _____. They would rather talk about mother earth than intimacy with _____ _____.

5

Buddhism

The Old New Age

So after sending two of those who assisted him, Timothy and Erastus, to Macedonia, he himself stayed in the province of Asia for a while.

During that time there was a major disturbance about the Way. For a person named Demetrius, a silversmith who made silver shrines of Artemis, provided a great deal of business for the craftsmen. When he had assembled them, as well as the workers engaged in this type of business, he said: "Men, you know that our prosperity is derived from this business. You both see and hear that not only in Ephesus, but in almost the whole province of Asia, this man Paul has persuaded and misled a considerable number of people by saying that gods made by hand are not gods! So not only do we run a risk that our business may be discredited, but also that the temple of the great goddess Artemis may be despised and her magnificence come to the verge of ruin—the very one whom the whole province of Asia and the world adore."

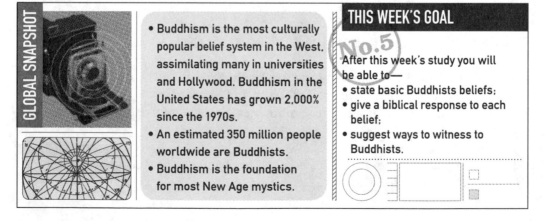

GLOBAL SNAPSHOT

- Buddhism is the most culturally popular belief system in the West, assimilating many in universities and Hollywood. Buddhism in the United States has grown 2,000% since the 1970s.
- An estimated 350 million people worldwide are Buddhists.
- Buddhism is the foundation for most New Age mystics.

THIS WEEK'S GOAL

No.5

After this week's study you will be able to—
- state basic Buddhists beliefs;
- give a biblical response to each belief;
- suggest ways to witness to Buddhists.

When they had heard this, they were filled with rage and began to cry out, "Great is Artemis of the Ephesians!" So the city was filled with confusion; and they rushed all together into the amphitheater, dragging along Gaius and Aristarchus, Macedonians who were Paul's traveling companions. Though Paul wanted to go in before the people, the disciples did not let him. Even some of the provincial officials of Asia, who were his friends, sent word to him, pleading with him not to take a chance by going into the amphitheater. Meanwhile, some were shouting one thing and some another, because the assembly was in confusion, and most of them did not know why they had come together. Then some of the crowd gave Alexander advice when the Jews pushed him to the front. So motioning with his hand, Alexander wanted to make his defense to the people. But when they recognized that he was a Jew, a united cry went up from all of them for about two hours: "Great is Artemis of the Ephesians!"

However, when the city clerk had calmed the crowd down, he said, "Men of Ephesus! What man is there who doesn't know that the city of the Ephesians is the temple guardian of the great Artemis, and of the image that fell from heaven? Therefore, since these things are undeniable, you must keep calm and not do anything rash. For you have brought these men here who are not temple robbers or blasphemers of our goddess. So if Demetrius and the craftsmen who are with him have a case against anyone, the courts are in session, and there are proconsuls. Let them bring charges against one another. But if you want something else, it must be decided in a legal assembly. In fact, we run a risk of being charged with rioting for what happened today, since there is no justification that we can give as a reason for this disorderly gathering." After saying this, he dismissed the assembly. Acts 19:22-41

The Skeleton Key of Modern Spiritualism

Recently on the West Coast a large crowd gathered to witness a typical Hollywood event. Celebrities of every stripe paraded past the crowds, who were feverishly taking pictures. As flashbulbs popped in syncopation, leaders in the business, entertainment, and music worlds waved. The event had the feel of a movie premiere or an opening night on Broadway. However, it was far from a mere studio publicity stunt; it was the opening of the newest Buddhist temple.

No other religion in the world has been as effectively repackaged to fit culture as Buddhism. On every continent it has been revised to meet specific cultural criteria and regional beliefs. There are Buddhist Muslims, Buddhist humanists, and even some erroneously called Buddhist Christians. Buddhism has rightly been called the old New Age, but it is also a chameleonic faith: it assumes the colors and shape of its immediate background. Buddhism can be credited for the advent of such cults as Scientology and Erhard Seminars Training (EST). Buddhism has become the skeleton key for our present cultural spiritualism.

As we examine Buddhism this week, you will quickly see that it is a system more difficult to definitively summarize than any other. It is as slippery as an eel and as complex as quantum physics. We can begin to solve the enigma by examining its historical roots and uncovering its central beliefs.

Day 1: Who Am I? God and Humanity

According to Acts 19:24-26, Demetrius had a vested interest in silencing Paul: " 'You know that our prosperity is derived from this business. You both see and hear that not only in Ephesus, but in almost the whole province of Asia ...' " (Acts 19:25-26). Demetrius's indictment before a meeting of the "metallurgy union" was a simple one: Paul was condemning all forms of worship except for the worship of Jesus Christ. He was " 'saying that gods made by hand are not gods' " (v. 26). In Ephesus stood one of the Seven Wonders of the world—the temple of Diana (known as Artemis to the Romans). Dedicated by the Greeks, it was a testament both to humanity's craftsmanship and to its paganism. Built in 550 B.C. of white marble, it burned to the ground in 356 B.C.

At this juncture Buddhism and our Scripture intersect. When the temple was rebuilt, the goddess within was also remodeled. The Greek Diana was a superwoman, a huntress of cosmic proportions. The rebuilt Diana, of whom Demetrius spoke, was decidedly different, carved as a divine mother, with an Asiatic design. Her torso was covered with many breasts, symbolizing her connection to life and nature. In Paul's day she had more in common with Hinduism than Greco-Roman mythology.

Classic Buddhism would in fact agree with Paul. To understand why, we need to explore the roots of this ancient religion.

Buddhism was born from Hinduism. The founder of Buddhism, Siddhartha Gautama, lived from 563 until 483 B.C. His father, Suddhodana, was a wealthy chieftain of the Shakya tribe in Kapilavastu in what was then the northeastern section of India (now part of Nepal). Siddhartha was reared as a faithful Hindu with every privilege of a nobleman.

As he reposed in a life of luxury, Siddhartha became discontented with what he perceived as the glaring deficiencies of Hinduism. Buddhist tradition teaches that in 534 B.C. Siddhartha wandered from his father's palace and was confronted with agonizing poverty, disease, and sickness among the lower classes of India.

This moment launched Siddhartha's spiritual quest. By depicting evil and suffering as a mere illusion, Hinduism was ignoring the anguished existence of the masses. Siddhartha believed that by claiming 330 million gods in a celestial pantheon, Hinduism was overly confusing and complex. Becoming disenchanted with his life and virtually everything he believed, he left his wife, his son, his ancestral home, and his wealth and became a wandering ascetic and seeker. For six years Siddhartha wandered. He meditated, he studied, and he questioned.

WITNESSING TIP

Explain That God Is Always Near

Buddhists reject the idea of a personal God. Because they believe in and fear spirits, they burn incense or offer food at home altars for protection. Share with them that God is a personal God who is always near, always around us, and always in us (see Jas. 4:8). Explain that God gives His followers real peace (see Phil. 4:7).

He virtually starved himself during his journeys and almost drowned while bathing because he was so weak. It became clear to him that the life of excessive simplicity was also not the answer to his quest.

Reaching the city of Bodh Gaya, Siddhartha sat down under a fig tree near a river and refused to rise again until he found the answer to life. He entered a deep meditative state and for 49 days meditated under the tree. In his trance Siddhartha battled with Mara, known in Hinduism as the evil one. Finally, after this prolonged struggle Siddhartha achieved enlightenment. He reached nirvana, which is the ultimate goal of both Hinduism and Buddhism, but the path he traveled was vastly different from traditional Hinduism.

Siddhartha became known as Buddha, and his teachings became the radical alternative to Hinduism. Rather than denying the existence of suffering, Siddhartha embraced it. Rather than seeking help from one of millions of gods, Siddhartha shifted his focus away from gods to the goal itself: nirvana. He called his method the Middle Way because it represented neither extreme indulgence nor extreme denial.

Siddhartha's discovery and method illustrate a profound difference between Hinduism and Buddhism. Although some Hindus are atheists, many believe in a god or gods. Buddhism, however, denies any personal god. Thus, Buddhists would agree with Paul on this point: the gods made by men are not gods. In fact, Buddhists believe in no divine being at all. God is not a *he* but at best a force or an energy. In Buddhism there is no god, but everyone and everything share a divine essence. We are all absorbed in the supernatural "stuff" that permeates everything.

Allow me to offer a simple illustration. My wife and my mother-in-law share a common gift: they can both cook a rock and make it delicious! As a Turk, I was not exposed to Southern cooking, but I quickly learned. However, there is one dimension of cooking that my mother-in-law cannot stand. She cannot tolerate frying fish inside the home. When fish is fried indoors, she notes, the smell is absorbed in every corner of the house. Your clothes, your hair, and even the curtains smell like fish.

This pervasive smell is similar to the Buddhist concept of the god-essence. Like the odor of fried fish, this essence is part of everything, living or inanimate. Everything shares this common "scent" that the Buddhist calls the soul. This teaching, called pantheism, achieves the same goal as Hinduism: both systems embrace vegetarianism and an organic lifestyle because all life shares a common essence.

Contrast Buddhism and Hinduism by writing *B, H,* or both letters in each blank.

_____ **1. Suffering is merely an illusion to be ignored.**

_____ **2. Suffering is to be embraced as the path to nirvana.**

_____ **3. No personal god exists.**

_____ **4. At least 330 million gods exist.**

_____ **5. Nirvana is the ultimate goal.**

DEFINITION

Pantheism

The belief that everything is God or a part of God

The correct answers are 1. H, 2. B, 3. B, 4. H, 5. B and H.

Differences Between Hinduism and Buddhism	
Hindus	**Buddhists**
Believe in millions of gods	Believe in no god or gods
Are likely to have small statues in home	Have no idols except maybe a Buddha
See a God force in everything	View humans as the only center
Are more likely to attract environmental activists due to belief in pantheism	Are more likely to attract intellectuals and philosophers

Confronting the Truth

Sounds confusing, doesn't it? We all share the same energy or life force, which is God? Human beings are the essential center of the universe and yet part of one large soul? Buddhism certainly doesn't offer much in the way of a personal relationship with God.

Our response to Buddhists should mirror Paul's proclamation in Acts 17:22-31, which we studied in week 2. Recall that this sermon caused Demetrius to organize a protest against Paul. In verses 24-25 Paul stated that there is one living God. Unlike the Buddhist picture of a massive divine soul, God is real and personal.

Read Acts 17:26 in the margin. What did Paul say is God's relationship to human beings?

_____

Buddhism devalues individuals because it sees them as part of a divine whole. Paul emphasized that God is not part of creation; He is the Creator. He determines our boundaries. He is Lord. Therefore, each person is a special creation and is made in God's image (see Gen. 1:27). Yet Paul did not stop there.

Underline God's command to all people in Acts 17:30 in the margin.

Paul stated that this God who is Lord and Creator wants all people everywhere to repent of their sins. Because repentance is the threshold of salvation, God is intimately involved with individuals. He values people so much that He offered His Son as a sacrifice for sin so that all who trust Him can have eternal life (see John 3:16; Rom. 5:8). God longs for people to enter a relationship with Him. This is a deeper and more meaningful salvation than a meager journey to nirvana. It meets men and women at the point of personal longing and need.

" 'From one man He has made every nation of men to live all over the earth and has determined their appointed times and the boundaries of where they live.' "
Acts 17:26

" 'Having overlooked the times of ignorance, God now commands all people everywhere to repent.' "
Acts 17:30

Check the statements that are true about the personal God of Christianity.
○ **God is an impersonal force.**
○ **God is real and personal.**
○ **God creates humans in His image.**
○ **God is distant from His creation.**
○ **God wants a relationship with each person.**
○ **God leaves it to us to earn our salvation.**
○ **God provided His Son as the means of salvation.**

Day 2: How Can I Know? Authority and Truth

Enter any Christian bookstore today, and you can easily become overwhelmed by the number of specialized target-audience Bibles: men's Bibles, women's Bibles, children's Bibles, teen Bibles, couples' Bibles, and many more. However, even with their different approaches or audiences, all of these Bibles have one common denominator: they all contain all of the books of the Old and New Testaments.

Buddhists' sacred texts and written authority present an interesting contrast. The diverse collection of Buddhist writings lacks the unifying message of our Christian Bible. Before we can satisfactorily answer the question "What are the holy books of Buddhism?" we must first ask, "Which sect of Buddhism?" Each has a specific set of books that govern its doctrines.

Theravada Buddhism: Orthodox Buddhists

For two hundred years after Buddha's death, Buddhism's thousands of followers were unified in one cohesive movement. However, around the third century B.C. a major question arose: can a person who has reached enlightenment then guide others toward the same goal? It is similar to this question for Christians: after I am saved, should I be concerned only about my spiritual walk or help others find Jesus?

The Buddhist community split into two groups:

1. The Theravada, believing enlightenment was possible only for a select few, responded that a Buddhist has no responsibility to help others.
2. The Mahayana, meaning *greater vehicle*, believed enlightenment is attainable for the greater proportion of humans. In compassion they would delay entering nirvana until they helped others.

The best way to differentiate between the two branches is the obvious application of their beliefs. Mahayana Buddhists actively teach and reach others. The Theravada, often very private about their religion, believe others are predestined not to be enlightened, so it is useless to help others. A strong parallel exists between the Mahayana and evangelical Christians, the Theravada and nonevangelicals.

Theravada, or classic, Buddhism, attempts to strictly follow the Buddha's original doctrines and teachings. The word *Theravada*, meaning *the way of the elders*, illustrates this sect's orthodox position. Its sacred book, called the *Tripitaka*, consists of Buddha's teachings and is considered the most accurate collection of his wisdom. This Buddhist sect is primarily found in Myanmar, Cambodia, Laos, Sri Lanka, and Thailand.

Mahayana Buddhism: The Greater Vehicle Progressives

When Buddhism splintered into two groups, the Mahayana, the progressive Buddhists, were the largest group and became known as the Greater Vehicle (*mahayana*). Rather than limit themselves simply to the teachings of the Buddha, the Mahayana seek wisdom from a myriad of sources. Their doctrines are influenced not only by the *Tripitaka* but also by other sources, such as the Hindu Vedas. Many new teachers, also known as enlightened beings, wrote books that were collected into the *Mahayana Sutras.* Shamanistic books, which emphasize a nature-worship mentality, and the *Tantra* (Buddhist sensuality) are also influential. Today Mahayana Buddhism is practiced primarily in China, Hong Kong, Japan, Taiwan, and Vietnam.

Vajrayanan Buddhism: The Dalai Lama

Vajrayanan, or Tantric, Buddhism has become popular in the West due to its emphasis on finding power and control through techniques and rituals. This highly sensual and mystical form of Buddhism is practiced primarily in Bhutan, Mongolia, and Tibet. In Tibet the leader is the Dalai Lama. Though he has lived in exile for decades, he is considered the 14th incarnation of Avalokiteshvara, the teacher of compassion.

Nichiren Shoshu Buddhism: Japanese Reformed Buddhism

Around A.D. 1253 a Japanese Buddhist named Nichiren Daishonin, believing he was the second Buddha, declared all Buddhist sects corrupt. His prolific writings, collected after his death in 1282, are called the *Gosho.* Along with the *Lotus Sutras*, these books form the basis for the movement. The *Lotus Sutras* are allegedly Gautama's actual, literal words that were recorded and translated. Nichiren Shoshu Buddhists are very strict and ritualistic in their devotion and practices.

The major emphasis of this movement is karma, the Hindu law of cause and effect. The priests chant long passages of the *Lotus Sutras* eight times a day and rub beads until they feel they have found peace.

This sect would not be considered a major faction of Buddhism except that it has experienced a resurgence in modern times. In 1930 a Buddhist teacher named Tsunesaburo Makiguchi renewed the movement and popularized it once again. It has truly found a foothold in Japan.

Zen Buddhism: Meditative Buddhism

The most interesting form of Buddhism and the most recognizable in the West is Zen Buddhism. The movement is interesting not only because of what it teaches but also for what it does not teach. Zen Buddhism has no sacred books, no central doctrines, and no organization to speak of. It is pure, unadulterated mysticism and existentialism, based entirely on meditation and mystical experience.

The Zen movement traces its foundation to Mahakasyapa, a supposed disciple of Buddha. The Buddha did not actually teach Mahakasyapa. Instead, he allegedly silently picked a flower and communicated telekinetically with his student. This unspoken language gave the movement the "doctrine of the Buddha mind." This secret knowledge enabled Mahakasyapa to reach awakening (*bodhi*) just like Buddha. The mode of achieving this awakening, or salvation, is meditation. Today Zen Buddhism is practiced primarily in parts of China and Japan, Western Europe, and America.

Match the five branches of Buddhism with the correct summary statements.

___ **1. Theravada**
    a. Progressives who added other teachers, the first group to split from classic Buddhism, evangelistic

___ **2. Mahayana**
    b. Meditative Buddhism, most recognized group in the West; individuals find their own path

___ **3. Vajrayanan**
    c. Japanese in origin, very strict and ritualistic, emphasizes karma and chanting

___ **4. Nichiren Shoshu**
    d. Strictly follows Siddhartha Gautama's original teachings and makes no effort to evangelize

___ **5. Zen**
    e. Led by the Dalai Lama, popular in the West, emphasizes gaining power and control

Confronting the Truth

Obviously, it is inconsistent and illogical to believe that every person picks and chooses his or her own truth. However, it is precisely this inconsistency that Buddhism embraces. Because someone's moment of enlightenment is not tied to objective truth and each person experiences it differently, Buddhists happily accept this contradiction. In fact, Buddhists seek the illogical and the contradictory because they regard logic and reason as prisons from which the mind must be released.

You should have answered 1. d, 2. a, 3. e, 4. c, 5. b.

Obviously, seeking to share the truth of Jesus with people who value illogic is difficult. From the information you have studied today, what flaw in the system can you lovingly point out to a follower of the Middle Way?

_____

Within the world of Buddhist sects we find a contradiction with which even they cannot live. If all truth is based on experience and all authority is personal, why would each sect claim to be more valid than the others? As we have already noted, the Japanese form of Buddhism, Nichiren Shoshu, declared all other sects of Buddhism invalid. How can such a judgment be possible if truth is completely subjective? If everyone is on the proper path to varying degrees because we are all on the same journey, then it is arrogant to believe that one person's authority is greater than anyone else's. It is also a renouncement of their own doctrine.

The answer, of course, is that truth is not subjective. God has disclosed universal truth in the divinely inspired Scriptures of the Old and New Testaments. They are the true and perfect record of God's revelation to humanity and of salvation through His Son, Jesus Christ (see 2 Tim. 3:15-17).

"No prophecy of Scripture comes from one's own interpretation, because no prophecy ever came by the will of man; instead, moved by the Holy Spirit, men spoke from God."
2 Peter 1:20-21

Read 2 Peter 1:20-21 in the margin.
The prophecy recorded in Scripture came from ○ *men* ○ *God.*
Therefore, Scripture contains ○ *subjective opinion* ○ *objective truth.*

Fulfilled prophecy shows the supernatural nature of God's Word. For example, Psalm 22 graphically describes Jesus' crucifixion, although it was written at least five hundred years before the Romans invented the cross. Can you think of two other examples of fulfilled prophecy about Jesus?

1. _____   2. _____

When a Christian approaches a Buddhist with the Bible, we do so with absolute assurance that only the Bible is supernatural and authoritative.

Day 3: Why Am I Here? Purpose and Ethics

Do you think Job could have embraced the prosperity gospel? This distortion of Christianity preaches a subtly deceptive message that can be summarized like this:

God wants to make you prosperous.
If you are not healthy, wealthy, or wise, it is due to your lack of faith.
Learn to speak wealth into existence and practice positive confession.
Don't claim an illness. God wants you to glorify Him when you are wealthy.

I doubt that Job, who suffered greatly in spite of being a righteous man, would have agreed with this "name it and claim it" philosophy. Certainly Paul would have differed with someone who claimed that the reason for his thorn in the flesh was his lack of faith! Almost every New Testament author wrote about the reality of trials in the Christian life; examples are James 1, 1 Peter 1, and Romans 8.

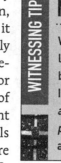

WITNESSING TIP

Make It Clear

When witnessing to Buddhists, avoid terms like *new birth, rebirth,* and *born again* because they will misunderstand you. Instead, use *endless freedom from guilt and sin, new power for living a holy life, promise of eternal life without suffering,* and *gift of unlimited merit.*

These trials bring us closer to God because they force us to rely on Him, as Paul wrote in 2 Corinthians 12:1-21. Instead of preaching a "believe it and achieve it" gospel, Paul says we are "to know Him [Christ] and the power of His resurrection and the fellowship of His sufferings, being conformed to His death" (Phil. 3:10).

That certainly doesn't sound like prosperity. It sounds as though we live in a fallen, diseased, and sin-sick world. It also sounds much more authentic. If we survey a world full of crimes, disease, pain, suffering, and injustice, we see that rain falls on the just and the unjust. Salvation in Christ doesn't make us immune to the effects of sin.

If you understand that concept, you can understand the origin of Buddhism. Born into a world of affluence and privilege, Gautama became dissatisfied with the unmitigated suffering around him. The very few who were wealthy and well fed, like himself, were outnumbered by the lowest caste of people, the Shudras (the peasant caste) and the Harijan (the outcastes who were called untouchable). The inequality was beyond Gautama's comprehension. Although he was a follower of Hinduism, all it seemed to offer was the dim hope of moving up a few stages or steps. To Gautama, Hinduism's most egregious offense was the preposterous Hindu notion that evil was an illusion.

During his seven-year nomadic existence, Gautama did not reject such essentials of Hinduism as reincarnation and karma; rather, he took a radically different approach to attaining the same end. He sought the same goal as Hinduism, nirvana, but the path would be a drastic detour. Unlike Hinduim, Buddhism does not ignore suffering; Buddhism embraces it. This is a critical concept in understanding Buddhism.

Buddha set forth his solution to suffering in the four Noble Truths, which dealt intimately with suffering and pain. He linked each one to a Buddhist's response and reaction, which are to be the purpose for the Buddhist's life and actions.

1. *The Truth of Suffering.* Life and existence are painful because they are tied to the cycles of birth, death, and rebirth. Suffering is inevitable.
2. *The Truth of the Cause of Suffering.* Suffering is caused by desire, which Buddha called craving. Desire, in turn, is caused by ignorance. Thus, Buddha identified a cause-and-effect cycle: ignorance causes desire, since we act only on instinct. Desire causes suffering, since we act only on our lowest instincts.

3. *The Truth of the Cessation of Suffering.* Suffering is destroyed when desire is rejected. Desire is rejected by means of knowledge and wisdom, which overcome ignorance. Once this journey is complete, Buddhists believe they have achieved nirvana—a state of bliss. Desire is obliterated, passion is controlled, and bliss is achieved.

4. *The Truth of the Path to the Cessation of Suffering.* The knowledge and wisdom needed to overcome ignorance are gained through the disciplines prescribed by the Eightfold Path:
   - Right understanding
   - Right thought
   - Right speech
   - Right action
   - Right livelihood
   - Right effort
   - Right mindfulness (awareness)
   - Right concentration (meditation)

We will study these disciplines as part of our discussion of salvation in day 5.

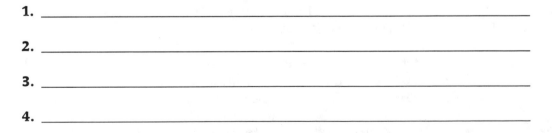

The Four Noble Truths

1. Suffering is real (*dukkha*).
2. Suffering is caused by desire (*samudaya*).
3. Suffering ends when desire ends (*nirodha*).
4. Desire ends by overcoming ignorance through the Eightfold Path (*magga*).

Imagine that you are a Buddhist. Based on what you have learned, write how you would describe each of the four Noble Truths to an inquirer.

1. _____

2. _____

3. _____

4. _____

Confronting the Truth

Buddha was uninterested in the philosophical or theological issues behind his teachings. In this sense Buddhism is intensely practical. For this reason Buddhism's moral principles are completely action-oriented. The modern picture of Buddhism as a deep philosophical system is deceptive, since Buddhism's primary cause and goal are the defeat of our passion (desire), which leads to suffering.

A Christian witness must understand two important points about Buddhists' purpose in life. First, a Buddhist does not see nirvana as a location, like God's abode. Second, Buddhism does not blame suffering on sin. Like Hinduism, Buddhism sees suffering as the product of human apathy and ignorance, not the result of sin. The warfare in Buddhism is between desire and enlightenment, not sin and salvation.

Pretend for a moment that you have a naturalist worldview with no God— a belief that nothing exists beyond the natural world. Which of the following would appeal to you as benefits of Buddhist thought?

○ **A way to end suffering**
○ **No interest in philosophical or theological issues**
○ **A concept of nirvana that is not a location like heaven**
○ **Humans as the center of existence**
○ **A plan to gain enlightenment and thus superiority**
○ **No objective concept of sin**

How does Christianity respond to the "benefits" you checked?

The issue of suffering is an important point of contact with Buddhists. The Bible teaches that humanity's primary problem is not suffering but sin. People sin by rebelling against God (see Ps. 51:4) and breaking His law (see 1 John 3:4), not through ignorance. All humankind is sinful by nature and is guilty before God (see Rom. 3:23). However, those who trust in Jesus Christ are forgiven (see 2 Cor. 5:19-21).

You can share the good news that those who trust Christ have spiritual resources for dealing with suffering. God participates in our suffering by helping us in our weakness (see Rom. 8:26), by giving us the Holy Spirit to intercede for us (see Rom. 8:26-27), by working in every situation for our good (see Rom. 8:28), and by promising that nothing can separate us from Him (see Rom. 8:35-39). A Christian also has the hope of a future life free of suffering. A Christian's hope for the afterlife is not extinction but conscious, meaningful, eternal fellowship with Christ in heaven (see 2 Cor. 4:18; Phil. 1:23), free of suffering and pain (see Rev. 21:4).

Day 4: Where Am I Going? Eternity and Legacy

Attracting Followers

Buddhism's view of eternity attracts many social activists and New Age followers.

1. Buddhists regard fighting social injustice as a sacred act.
2. Because peace is found through meditation, Buddhists place great value on working for peace in society.
3. Ultimately, Buddhism is not interested in eternity, instead preferring to invest its energy in peace activism and social causes.
4. The Buddhist doctrine of reincarnation lends itself to these New Age teachings: past-life regression, spirit teachers, and energy focus (*shakra*).
5. The Buddhist focus on internal energy forces offers New Age teachers opportunities to seek a higher state of consciousness through such practices as crystals, divining rods, and spiritual massages.

All branches of Buddhism seek enlightenment. Though the process is often slow, Buddhists see this as the only means of progress on their journey. To gain wisdom for the journey toward enlightenment, Buddhists follow a structured, philosophical path that is guided by wise teachers and is governed by the immutable law of karma. If they do good, in whatever way they define good, they will receive good and become good. If they do evil, they increase suffering in their lives. This ethic is called *sila*, or moral precepts. Their entire journey is consumed by *sila*.

This cycle (*samsara*) is eventually defeated by abandoning desire. Once desire is gone, suffering dissipates. Once suffering is overcome, Buddhists are released from the prison of life and lose themselves in the great, vast expanse of nothingness called nirvana. Nirvana, which means *blown out* or *extinct,* is not a place but a state of bliss in which the Buddhist is free from the agonizing cycle of death and reincarnation. Unlike heaven, nirvana is not a conscious state but extinction. Those who reach nirvana simply stop existing. Buddha described this "salvation" in the *Pali Sutras:*

> There is a sphere which is neither earth, nor water, nor fire, nor air, which
> is not the sphere of the infinity of space, nor the sphere of the infinity of
> consciousness, the sphere of nothingness, the sphere of perception. ...
> I deny that it is coming or going, enduring death or birth. It is only the
> end of suffering.

Does this clarify Buddhist eternity for you? Probably not! Buddhism is as vague about eternity as it is about existence. You, as an individual, do not exist in any real way, so why would you continue forever? Nirvana, it would seem, is pure nonexistence.

Check the Buddhist beliefs to complete the following statements.

The central problem in life is to ○ *please God* ○ *alleviate suffering.*
The solution can be found in ○ *abandoning desire* ○ *loving God.*
Nirvana is the bliss of ○ *relationships with God and others*
   ○ *meaningful work* ○ *nonexistence.*

We can summarize the Buddhist view of eternity like this:
1. Nothing is permanent (*annica*).
2. You do not really exist (*anatta*).
3. Karma, good or bad, determines whether you reincarnate up or down the chain.
4. Once you truly deny your existence (desire), you extinguish the flame of life.
5. Then you reach nirvana and simply cease to be.
So to our question "Where are you going?" Buddhists would answer with a sly smile, "Nowhere, and neither are you." Because Buddhists seek the obliteration of self, the Christian concept of eternal life is foreign to them.

Confronting the Truth

Recently, many Buddhists have attempted to prove that the Bible affirms reincarnation, citing Jesus' use of "born again" in John 3:7. When Nicodemus asked Jesus whether he had to physically go through another cycle of life, he articulated the Buddhist misconception of salvation and eternity. Jesus corrected him, noting that this rebirth is spiritual, not physical (see John 3:1-21).

The biblical view of eternity offers life, hope, and meaning.

Read the verses in the margin and match references with summary statements.

___ 1. Genesis 1:27
___ 2. Romans 8:28
___ 3. 1 Corinthians 15:52
___ 4. Hebrews 9:27
___ 5. Revelation 21:3-4

a. Eternity will mean living with God forever without suffering.
b. God works for the good of those who are His.
c. Humans have a definite beginning.
d. The body will be raised from death to life.
e. We live only one life on earth.

The Bible clearly stipulates that people die just one time and are then judged (see Heb. 9:27). An individual has not always existed, and neither does he travel on a cycle of birth and reincarnation. Genesis 1–2 teaches that humans have a definite beginning, and Revelation 21–22 details our eternal existence in this one glorified body. First Corinthians 15:51-57 adds that this body will be raised again. How is that possible if we are destined for many other forms of existence? In which body will our soul exist? Christians know that the moral force governing the universe is not the law of karma but a personal God who has mercy on those who repent and works for the good of those who follow Christ (see Rom. 8:28).

"God created man in His own image; He created him in the image of God; He created them male and female."
Genesis 1:27

"We know that all things work together for the good of those who love God: those who are called according to his purpose."
Romans 8:28

"The trumpet will sound, and the dead will be raised incorruptible, and we will be changed."
1 Corinthians 15:52

"It is appointed for people to die once—and after this, judgment." Hebrews 9:27

"God's dwelling is with men, and He will live with them. They will be His people, and God Himself will be with them and be their God. He will wipe away every tear from their eyes. Death will exist no longer; grief, crying, and pain will exist no longer, because the previous things have passed away."
Revelation 21:3-4

The correct answers to the activity are 1. c, 2. b, 3. d, 4. e, 5. a.

Instead of the Buddhist's prospect of eventual annihilation, a Christian can offer a Buddhist true hope for the future. Those who place their trust in Jesus Christ are assured of eternal life in a new heaven and a new earth. This conscious, personal relationship with Christ will be forever free of suffering and pain.

Day 5: Is There Any Hope? Salvation and Security

One of my favorite confrontations was with a Zen Buddhist. After speaking at a midwestern university's student forum, I began to take questions from the audience. Because I have spent much of my life being yelled at, I have grown accustomed to being called all kinds of names. However, on this particular day the vitriolic response of a young 20-year-old was indeed memorable.

He said: "You are so arrogant! You Christians come here and tell us we are wrong, but you hypocrites never have peace! We are the peaceful ones!" As he was yelling, his face was turning bright red.

I said: "So how does this peace play out in your life? You don't even sound like a Buddhist."

Almost beside himself with rage, he stood to his feet and exclaimed: "See? You are a bigot! You think you know the only way! Buddhism has taught me peace and the ability to love my neighbor, you @#$%!"

I quietly asked him, "Am I your neighbor?"

"Yes!" he yelled.

"So why are you screaming at me?"

An audible "Ooohhhhh" rose from the audience. He sat down.

Though his youthful exuberance betrayed his philosophy, at least the young man understood the basic tenets of Buddhism. Buddha's fourth and final Noble Truth identified eight steps for overcoming desire and suffering and thereby reaching nirvana. The Eightfold Path can be divided into three major categories.

Salvation by Wisdom: Panna
Step 1: right understanding
Step 2: right thought

These two foundational steps are internal resolutions and discoveries that enable Buddhists to view themselves and others through a new system of thought. To change our actions, Buddhists teach, we must first change the way we think.

Salvation by Good Works: Sila
Step 3: right speech
Step 4: right action
Step 5: right livelihood

The hope of Buddhism is that the individual Buddhist will become selfless since he now understands he is on a journey to pure nothingness. He learns, therefore, to speak well of others, respond kindly to others, and live by a code of conduct that awaits retribution (karma).

Salvation by Mental Discipline: Samadhi
Step 6: right effort
Step 7: right mindfulness (awareness)
Step 8: right concentration (meditation)

These final three steps do not deal with action but with personal deportment. Right effort enables Buddhists to avoid evil thoughts, right awareness focuses on the good things they have done or attempted, and right meditation is the vehicle through which they can chant themselves into nirvana.

Fill in the blanks to review the three categories in the Eightfold Path.

1. **Wisdom consists of right _____ and right _____.**

2. **Works consist of right _____, right _____, and right _____.**

3. **Mental discipline consists of right _____, right _____, and right _____.**

Confronting the Truth

Like Hinduism, Buddhism teaches that the goodness needed to escape suffering and reach nirvana can be achieved by human effort. Progress on the path to enlightenment is achieved through good works, charity, and kindness. This concept is a strong bridge into the life of a Buddhist.

The Bible teaches that humans cannot do enough to earn favor. We cannot work our way to salvation. Show the Buddhist the central truth of Christ's atonement. If it were possible to achieve enough goodness to outweigh our badness and move upward, the evil deeds, motives, and

---

WITNESSING TIP

Make a Difference

Use commonalities with Buddhists to build a bridge for witness. Buddhists are to be commended for their work for social justice, but be careful to explain to the Buddhist that these actions do not earn salvation. Christians believe in fighting for the rights of the downtrodden, but this is a result of our salvation, not a means of earning it. Jesus taught His followers to have compassion for the poor and to minister to their needs, but He came to bring eternal spiritual redemption to people, not solely to meet physical needs on earth.

works would remain. In all works-centered religions a person's evil deeds go unpunished as long as the person eventually does more good than bad. In Buddhist thought, evil is simply forgotten.

This is not justice. In true justice Christ's death paid for our sin. Sins are not merely forgotten. Sins are purged from our debt. In the cosmic courthouse someone has to pay for these sins. Jesus Christ paid for the sin debt with His shed blood.

On the other hand, this is injustice because Jesus Himself never sinned. Show Buddhists that Buddha first had to conquer his own desire. Jesus, however, died as an innocent Lamb for the criminals—us. Look at Demetrius's accusation against Paul in Ephesus: " '... that the temple of the great goddess Artemis may be despised and her magnificence come to the verge of ruin' " (Acts 19:27). He said that Paul was making Artemis despised. Why would that be the result? Because through His blood Jesus proved that people cannot work their way into heaven. Christ died to extend mercy and grace. Only His blood can save.

> ## WITNESSING TIP
> ### Share Your Testimony
>
> Buddhists emphasize personal experience rather than doctrine. Share your personal testimony, emphasizing the change Christ has brought in your life. State what it means to have a personal relationship with Jesus, being sure to point out your freedom from guilt and assurance of heaven. Explain that only a relationship with Christ makes a person righteous before God. This is good news to a Buddhist who is struggling to break the cycles of karma and reincarnation.

Christians should be prepared to respond to Buddhists' three primary objections to salvation through Jesus Christ.

19 "In Christ, God was reconciling the world to Himself, not counting their treaspasses against them. 21He made the One who did not know sin to be sin for us, so that we might become the righteousness of God in Him."
2 Corinthians 5:19,21

1. Buddhists reject the concept of grace.
Most Buddhists see grace as a foreign concept altogether. Because each person must make his own way on the path of enlightenment, Buddhists wonder why Jesus' existence affects them in any way. Wasn't He dealing with His own salvation? Show them that grace is the only way by which we could ever approach God. Grace is not only the enlightenment of the mind but also the salvation of a person's entire being—body, mind, and soul.

Read 2 Corinthians 5:19,21. What does verse 19 say about God's gift of grace?
○ **Allows us to work out our salvation with fear and trembling**
○ **Doesn't count our sins against us**
○ **Calls all people everywhere to repent**

How does verse 21 describe Christ's part in delivering us from our sin?

2. Buddhists see Jesus' death as a violation of karma.

Buddhists object that if Jesus did all the Bible teaches He did, His death was the ultimate injustice rather than true justice. The Bible teaches, however, that Jesus' death was justice (see 2 Cor. 5:14-15).

True, Jesus was the just dying unjustly, but He was dying for us. He bore God's wrath and paid the just punishment for all sin (see 1 John 2:2). This is the purest form of justice because sin is not recycled through reincarnation; sin is redeemed through complete payment.

3. Buddhists reject the concept of personal worth.

The Bible teaches that every individual—even the lowest caste—has worth and is worthy of God's complete attention. Christ died for him personally. Buddhists aren't doomed to be annihilated into nothingness. Rather, they can choose to live eternally in heaven with the personal, intimate Redeemer who loves them inestimably.

What event, circumstance, or Scripture has most powerfully made you realize how much God values you?

_____

_____

Christianity offers true answers for the entire scope of Buddhism. Suffering will end one day when we reach heaven. Suffering exists because of sin, and people suffer without salvation. Christ's death shows humanity's infinite worth, and He is Lord even to the untouchables. We must clearly present Christ's uniqueness as the only true Savior and the personal nature of God.

In a most profound way, Jesus is the only *Bodhisattva* (guide and teacher) because only He can reach between humans and God and free people from their slavery to sin. People do not merely seek enlightenment; they seek meaning and purpose. These are found only in the forgiveness Christ offers.

Review the comparison chart on page 102 and summarize these Buddhist beliefs as if you were explaining them to a Buddhist friend.

God: _____

Sin: _____

Salvation: _____

"If One died for all, then all died. And He died for all so that those who live should no longer live for themselves, but for the One who died for them and was raised."
2 Corinthians 5:14-15

"He Himself is the propitiation for our sins, and not only for ours, but also for those of the whole world."
1 John 2:2

Review the witnessing tips in this week's material. Check one thing you will do this week to reach Buddhists in your sphere of influence.

○ **Learn more about Buddhist beliefs**
○ **Learn about Buddhists living in your community**
○ **Pray for the salvation of Buddhists**
○ **Develop a relationship with a Buddhist you know**
○ **Other:** _____

A Comparison of Beliefs

	Christianity	Buddhism
God	God is real and personal.	No god exists.
Humans	Each person, of infinite worth, is created in God's image.	We are a collection of one force and are insignificant as individuals.
Sin	We suffer because we are born sinners. Sin is directly against a righteous God and alienates us from Him.	We suffer because of desire.
Salvation	Ultimate hope is forgiveness by God and reconciliation through Christ's shed blood.	Ultimate hope is to reach nonexistence, which is nirvana.
The Means of Salvation	Salvation comes only by grace through faith in the Lord Jesus Christ. We do nothing to earn His love or salvation.	Enlightenment through the knowledge of the four Noble Truths on the Eightfold Path. Achieved through good works.
Eternity	We will live eternally with the triune God in heaven.	Nirvana is the end of reincarnation and of existence.

Viewer Guide
Group Session 5

Review Segment: Buddhism

Buddhism is _____.

Buddhism sees _____ as mother of all of us as part of God.

Buddhism is _____-centered and denies the existence of God.

Buddhist thinking:
If all of us are a part of a large essence of divine, then you need to
_____ _____ _____ with that, not pray to it.

In Hinduism and Buddhism they are _____ _____
_____ , confusing intentionally.

Many people get tired of the fog. They would rather embrace _____
with a standard: the cross.

Teaching Segment: Judaism: The Hollow Easter Bunny

Approximately 30 percent of Israeli Jews are _____. For many, being
Jewish is _____.

Even conservative, orthodox Jews do not practice the _____ system.

Some Reform Jews have stopped looking for the _____.
They observe high holy days but don't believe in the _____ who gave
them.

You know more about _____ than the average contemporary Jew.
For them, Judaism is a _____.

Approaching your Jewish friend:
- Continue your understanding of _____ Judaism.
- Build a _____.

When you remove your _____ with the God who created you,
all you have left is _____.

Jews are people for whom Christ _____, and they don't understand
the God that made them and the _____ He has with their people.

6 Judaism

The Hollow Easter Bunny

When the governor motioned to him to speak, Paul replied: "Because I know you have been a judge of this nation for many years, I am glad to offer my defense in what concerns me. You are able to determine that it is no more than 12 days since I went up to worship in Jerusalem. And they didn't find me disputing with anyone or causing a disturbance among the crowd, either in the temple complex or in the synagogues, or anywhere in the city. Neither can they provide evidence to you of what they now bring against me. But I confess this to you: that according to the Way, which they call a sect, so I worship my fathers' believing all the things that are written in the Law and in the Prophets. And I have a hope in God, which these men themselves also accept, that there is going to be a resurrection, both of the righteous and the unrighteous. I always do my best to have a clear conscience toward God

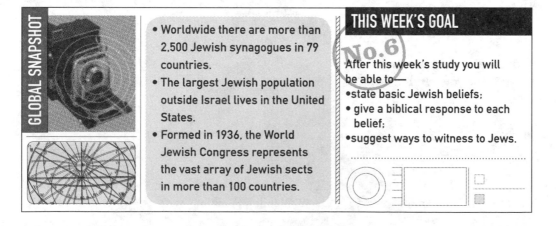

GLOBAL SNAPSHOT

- Worldwide there are more than 2,500 Jewish synagogues in 79 countries.
- The largest Jewish population outside Israel lives in the United States.
- Formed in 1936, the World Jewish Congress represents the vast array of Jewish sects in more than 100 countries.

THIS WEEK'S GOAL

No.6

After this week's study you will be able to—

- state basic Jewish beliefs;
- give a biblical response to each belief;
- suggest ways to witness to Jews.

and men. After many years, I came to bring charitable gifts and offerings to my nation, and while I was doing this, some Jews from the province of Asia found me ritually purified in the temple, without a crowd and without any uproar. It is they who ought to be here before you to bring charges, if they have anything against me. Either let these men here state what wrongdoing they found in me when I stood before the Sanhedrin, or about this one statement I cried out while standing among them, 'Today I am being judged before you concerning the resurrection of the dead.'"
Acts 24:10-21

Decorated, Empty Shells

I consider it one of the greatest disappointments of my young Christian life. Having watched Christians for a number of years, I had always secretly envied Christian children who would get huge chocolate Easter bunnies. As a Muslim, of course, I did not participate in Easter celebrations. Yet from a distance I would covet those chocolate bunnies. I imagined them as one- or two-pound blocks of pure delight.

The first Easter after my salvation, I discovered the shocking truth. Even though the bunnies appeared to be rock-solid and weighty, they were in fact hollow. They were beautifully crafted, immaculately decorated, and deceptively weighted shells. But they were empty.

It may come as a surprise to you that evangelical and Israel-loving Christians know more about the intricacies of the Jewish faith than the average Jewish person. In fact, after I began speaking out in support of Israel, one of the most ardent antagonists I faced was a Jewish theologian. My support, he stated, was based on a misplaced and misguided allegiance to the Old Testament.

For those who passionately want to reach their Jewish friends, this single point may be the largest stumbling block. The vast majority of the more than 14 million Jews on earth have abandoned the faith of their fathers. Like Paul speaking before Felix, you will be misunderstood. Like Paul, you must redouble your efforts to reach your friends. The Jewish world is the least connected and the most complex mingling of people in our study. Keep this fact in mind as we explore the Jewish world this week.

Day 1: Who Am I? God and Humanity

An old Jewish proverb teaches that if seven Jewish men are in a city, there will be six synagogues. As Paul discovered in his missionary journeys, the Jewish world has a splintered internal history. In Jesus' day there were four major groups of Jews: the Pharisees, the Sadducees, the Zealots, and the Essenes. Each group varied greatly in doctrine and practice, and each had its own particular view of God and humanity.

This pattern has continued throughout Jewish history. We will identify the seven major sects of modern Judaism. Knowing the differences in belief between these groups radically affects your approach to sharing the gospel of Christ with them.

Secular Judaism

Many people with Jewish lineage have virtually no connection to a Jewish community. They do not attend a Jewish center or synagogue. They do not celebrate *shabbats* (sabbaths) or follow the kosher dietary laws. They are Jewish by birth, not by practice. They identify themselves as Jewish as a means to preserve their heritage. They are uninterested in any conception of a God or salvation.

Kabbalah: Hindu-Judaic Mysticism

The most culturally popular form of Judaism today is based on medieval mysticism. The current popularity is due to the centers founded by Philip Berg. Kabbalists call Rabbi Berg the Rav, and many consider him the "living conduit between the light and the creator."[1] The movement is highly superstitious; adherents wear a red thread as a bracelet, drink Kabbalah-blessed water to cure diseases, and run their hands over a text instead of reading it to understand the deeper meanings. Any belief in a definable God is vague because it is intentionally indistinct, mixing Hindu mysticism and practices with Jewish texts and prayers. The movement has been around for hundreds of years, beginning as a movement called *Qabalah* (Hebrew for *receiving*).

Reconstructionist Judaism (Evolutionary Judaism)

Mordecai Kaplan founded this movement as an alternative for nonreligious and secular Jews. While followers embrace their cultural heritage and strongly support Israel, they speak in terms of spirituality rather than doctrinal beliefs or a concept of God. As reconstructionists are often fond of saying, people take precedence over doctrine. Any interpretation of God is supplanted by progressive social involvement. Followers study the *Torah* (written law) alongside modern philosophies. Sin is not defined, and God is seen as the Life, Love, and Intelligence of the universe.

Reform Judaism

The largest sect of Judaism in North America is the Reform movement. Founded by Rabbi Isaac Mayer Wise in 1873, it now claims more than nine hundred congregations.[2] Worldwide, followers make up 22 percent of the Jewish population. The movement attempts to take seriously the core beliefs in the Torah and Israel, but it is very liberal in its support of homosexuality, feminism, and agnosticism.

Conservative Judaism

Though the name would suggest otherwise, Conservative Judaism is not an orthodox branch but rather a bridge between the orthodox and liberal sects of Judaism. The name applies more to followers' ethics and practice than their beliefs. They attempt to conserve some of the traditional and historical Jewish practices, such as observing the *shabbat*, but they do not necessarily adhere to the biblical meanings behind those rituals. This sect is the most varied and diverse Jewish sect, with some holding a strong biblical understanding of God and others leaning more to Reform doctrine.

Match the five sects of modern Judaism we have considered so far.

___ **1. Secular**	**a. Mixes a Hindu worldview with Judaism**
___ **2. Kabbalah**	**b. Practices spirituality without defined teachings**
___ **3. Reconstructionist**	**c. Observes traditional Jewish practices but not**
___ **4. Reform**	**necessarily the biblical meanings**
___ **5. Conservative**	**d. Attempts to embrace both the *Torah* and a**
	liberal social agenda
	e. Jewish only to preserve their heritage

I hope you matched the groups this way: 1. e, 2. a, 3. b, 4. d, 5. c. Let's look at two more pieces in the mosaic of modern Judaism.

Orthodox Judaism

Of all the sects of modern Judaism, the two orthodox sects are most in line with the traditional and biblical understandings of Judaism. Orthodox Judaism is a very academic movement that demands a conversion and believes in the covenant with the God of Israel (*b'rit*). Followers believe in the God of Abraham, Isaac, Jacob, and Joseph and explicitly follow the teachings of the *Torah*. They observe the *shabbat* every week and intensely study the teachings.

Ultraorthodox Judaism

Perhaps the most recognizable form of Judaism is the Hasidic sect. As often portrayed in the media, the Hasidim wear black or grey suits and the skullcap (*yarmulke*). Interestingly, the Hasidim are more mystical than the Orthodox and often study Kabbalah. However, they are equally committed to the traditional doctrines and teachings of Judaism about God and humanity.

As you can imagine from this overview of the primary sects, it is extremely difficult to give a comprehensive answer to any doctrinal issue in Judaism because modern Jews vary from atheistic secularists to orthodox Hasidim. For our purposes we will focus on traditional Judaism.

To discern the Jewish understanding of God, it is helpful to read Paul's response when he appeared before Felix to face the accusations of the Jewish community.

Read Acts 24:14-15 in the margin and check what Paul said about God.
○ **Paul denied that the Jews believed in the God of the Old Testament.**
○ **Paul stated that the Jews believed in the God of the Old Testament.**

Paul explicitly affirmed the Jews' belief in the God of the Old Testament. The Jewish concept of God is based on Deuteronomy 6:4-9: " 'Listen, Israel: The Lord our God, the Lord is One. Love the Lord your God with all your heart, with all your soul, and with all your strength.' " This is called the *Sh'ema Yisrael*. He is the Holy One of Israel, and His name is too holy even to speak. God's self-identification in Exodus 3:14 to Moses

" 'I confess this to you. ... I worship my fathers' God, believing all the things that are written in the Law and in the Prophets. And I have a hope in God, which these men themselves also accept, that there is going to be a resurrection, both of the righteous and the unrighteous.' "
Acts 24:14-15

is considered so sacred that devout Jews will not even write it, often writing "G-d." This God, the Creator of heaven and earth, has revealed Himself to the prophets of the Hebrew Scriptures. God is personal, holy, and just.

The Hebrew word denoting God's oneness is *echad*, which refers to a composite unity. Modern Jews, however, interpret God's unity as an absolute, unqualified oneness that does not allow for a trinitarian view of God. Perhaps you have heard the argument that modern Jews do not worship the same God as Christians because they deny His triune nature. Is this true?

How did Paul answer that question in Acts 24:14-15? _____

_____

Paul did not agree that modern Jews do not worship the same God as Christians. He argued that Jews who had accepted Jesus were worshiping the God of their fore-fathers—the God of Abraham, Isaac, and Jacob. In fact, the Messianic Jewish move-ment is based on the concept that Messianic Jews (Christians from Jewish lineage) are completed Jews. They have accepted Jesus (Yeshua) as the Messiah and God-Man; they have come full circle from expecting the Messiah, to seeing Him and accepting His advent, to finally expecting His second coming. Like Paul, we can share with Jews that those who accept Christ are affirming a belief in the trinitarian God revealed in the Old Testament Law, Prophets, and Writings.

What do Jews believe about humanity? Judaism holds that people are basically good because they bear God's image. Although humans don't have a sinful nature, they nonetheless have the capacity to choose sinful, evil acts. Jewish people commonly think of sin in terms of almost criminal behavior. Usually, they would not consider themselves to be sinners because they do not possess a sinful nature. This position does not recognize the need for humanity's restoration, especially with respect to the Jewish people. Because Jews don't believe that people are separated from God, they don't see the need for the good news.

Confronting the Truth

Christians must affirm the triune nature of God as revealed in Scripture (see Gen. 1:26; Isa. 48:12-16). True to the meaning of the Hebrew word *echad*, we believe that God has revealed Himself as Father, Son, and Holy Spirit; yet He is one God. Christians believe that the God of the Old and New Testaments is the same.

Christians cannot accept the Jewish view of humanity as basically good. We affirm humanity's creation in God's image, but we also believe in humanity's fall and its need for salvation (see Gen. 3). The Hebrew Scriptures emphasize the fact of our sinful condition and the need for atonement. For these reasons it is imperative that we reach Jews with the gospel of Jesus Christ.

Read the verses in the margin from the Jewish Scriptures and describe what each says about the nature of humans.

Genesis 6:5: _____

Ecclesiastes 9:3: _____

Isaiah 53:6: _____

"The Lord saw that man's wickedness was widespread on the earth and that every scheme his mind thought of was nothing but evil all the time."
Genesis 6:5

"This is an evil in all that is done under the sun: there is one fate for everyone. In addition, the hearts of people are full of evil, and madness is in their hearts while they live."
Ecclesiastes 9:3

"We all went astray like sheep; we all have turned to our own way."
Isaiah 53:6

Focusing on common beliefs about God can help Christians reach sincere Jews. We wholeheartedly agree with the orthodox understanding of God as Creator and Sustainer and as being personal and holy. Old Testament references to the Lord's fatherly provision, such as in Psalm 23, also carry a redemptive message. The Shepherd always provides for His sheep.

Many Jews sometimes resist Christians because they see us as pushy or brash. A gentle heart and a warm disposition certainly open more doors than the expected Bible thumping. We should not be perceived as a threat to Judaism but a friend.

WITNESSING TIP

Respond to Suspicion

Most Jews are suspicious of Christians because throughout history Jews have been persecuted and forced to convert to a variety of religions. "Christian" movements such as the Crusades and the Inquisitions subjected Jews to brutal torture. If a Jew brings up these topics, explain it is unfair to equate medieval Roman Catholics with evangelical Christians today. Baptists played a key role in bringing religious liberty to America, and few groups have benefited more than Jewish people. Be especially humble to offset the perception that Christians are an arrogant majority.

DEFINITION

Halakhah

Jewish law, consisting of commandments from the Torah and customs adopted by the rabbis

Day 2: How Can I Know? Authority and Truth

I once heard a well-intentioned Christian attempt to witness to a Jewish man by asking him whether he believed in the Old Testament. Though the man would have answered yes, he instead walked away angry, having been insulted by the Christian's word choice. To Jews, there is no Old Testament. They do not accept the New Testament as Scripture. They know our Old Testament as the *Torah* or the *Tanakh*.

The Jewish authority for life is not simply a set of doctrines or beliefs. It is called *halakhah*, which means *Jewish law*. It is a comprehensive way of life, filled with rules that affect every aspect of life: prayer, diet, clothing, hygiene, marriage, and doctrine. *Halakhah* is a collection of *mitzvot* (commandments) from the *Torah* as well as customs adopted by the rabbis. All of these laws are considered Jewish law and are equally binding. Therefore, a devout Jew has two components of authority for truth, life, and teachings: (1) the written law, known as the *Torah* or *Tanakh*, and (2) the oral law, known as the *Talmud* and *Mishnah*.

Circle each statement *T* for *true* or *F* for *false*.

T	F	1. Judaism is primarily a set of beliefs.
T	F	2. The written law is known as the *Torah* or *Tanakh*.
T	F	3. The Jewish law includes rules that affect every area of life.
T	F	4. Jews accept certain New Testament books as authoritative.

Statements 1 and 4 are false, while 2 and 3 are true.

DEFINITION

Torah or Tanakh
Written law

Talmud and Mishnah
Oral law

The Written Authority: Torah

The word *Torah* means *law* in Hebrew. With only a few variations in translation, the *Torah* corresponds to our Old Testament. However, because Jews derive the names of the books from Hebrew, their names are different from our English/Latin titles. The Hebrew written *Torah* is divided into three sections: the Law (*Torah*), the Prophets (*Nevi'im*), and the Writings (*Kethuvim*). In the Pentateuch (the first five books of the Bible) the name of each book comes from the first Hebrew words in the book. The word *Tanakh* is simply the first letters of these three Hebrew categories of Scripture (*Tnk*).

The Oral Authority: Talmud and Mishnah

In addition to the written Scriptures, devout Jews also have the oral law, known as the *Talmud*. The *Talmud* is a collection of wise sayings by devout rabbis, who explained how the *Torah* was to be interpreted and applied. Once these sayings and teachings were collected in written form in the second century A.D., they became known as the *Mishnah*.

Each sect of Judaism has certain rabbis and certain *Mishnah* to which they adhere more closely than others. For example, some sects, such as the Orthodox and the Hasidic, take teachings on clothing more seriously than the other sects. Similarly, some Jews pray in a certain manner, while others are not as stringent about form.

In addition, sects often add other books to their core teachings to lend wider authority. For example, the Kabbalah movement includes two books, *Sepher Yetzirah* (the book of creation) and *Zohar* (the book of splendor), enabling adherents to cite teachings in those books that are fundamental to the beliefs of the sect. These mystical books use numerology and magic to explain the search for hidden meanings beneath the actual text.

Match the Jewish sources of authority with their meanings.

___ 1. *Halakhah*	a. Oral law recorded in writing
___ 2. *Torah* or *Tanakh*	b. Oral law
___ 3. *Talmud*	c. Jewish law, consisting of commandments
___ 4. *Mishnah*	from the *Torah* and customs adopted by the rabbis
	d. Written law

The correct answers are 1. c, 2. d, 3. b, 4. a.

Let's return to the example of the Apostle Paul's evangelism to Jews whose beliefs differed. In Acts 21 a hostile Jewish crowd confronted Paul. They too were divided in their allegiances and authority, since some were Pharisees and others were allied with the Sadducees. Yet Paul began his preaching by emphasizing the Jewish nature of the gospel. Citing his own Jewish training, he proclaimed Jesus as the fulfillment of the Jewish quest for the Messiah. In Acts 22 he spoke in Hebrew to gather their interest (see v. 2), cited his rearing and training by Gamaliel (see v. 3), and clearly stated that the One he saw in a vision was the " 'God of our fathers' " (see v. 14). Later in his defense before Felix, he emphasized that he believed all things " 'that are written in the Law and in the Prophets' " (Acts 24:14).

WITNESSING TIP

Enter Their World

Attend a synagogue or temple service with your Jewish friend. Ask questions. Find out why the participants face the same way or why men and women sit apart. You may then have an opportunity to explain the components of Christian worship services. Both services attempt to reconcile sinful people to the holy God. Explain the symbols in a church, such as the baptistry (Hebrew *mikvat*) and the altar. While we understand these elements in a different way, they are useful visual aids in promoting dialogue and in witnessing.

What was the purpose of Paul's approach outlined above?
○ **Paul tried to confuse his audience.**
○ **Paul appealed to beliefs that all Jews held in common.**
○ **Paul wanted the Jews to like him.**

In spite of the different beliefs that existed among the listeners in his audience, Paul wisely appealed to a set of beliefs that all of these Jews held in common.

What fundamental beliefs unite Jews today that would enable us to discuss issues of faith? This is a difficult question because modern Jewish sects dispute any dogma as authoritative. One widely accepted source, however, is Maimonides, a hero of medieval Jewish faith. Known as Rabbi Moshe ben Maimon, he identified 13 core essentials for the Jewish community. This collection, known as Rambam's 13 Principles of Faith, although very general and basic, serves as a launching point for Christians who want to discuss common Jewish beliefs in a context of radical diversity.

Rambam's 13 Principles of Faith

1. God exists.
2. God is one and unique.
3. God is incorporeal (without a physical body).
4. God is eternal.
5. Prayer is to be directed to God alone and to no other.
6. The words of the prophets are true.
7. Moses' prophecies are true, and Moses was the greatest of the prophets.
8. The written *Torah* (the first five books of the Bible) and the oral *Torah* (*Talmud*) were given to Moses.
9. There will be no other *Torah*.
10. God knows the thoughts and deeds of people.
11. God will reward the good and punish the wicked.
12. The Messiah will come.
13. The dead will be resurrected.

Review the 13 principles of faith and check those you believe as a Christian.

Christians can actually endorse most of these. You might question number 5 until you remember that both Jesus and the Holy Spirit are God. God the Father and the Spirit are incorporeal, but in Jesus, God took on human flesh. And while Moses holds a place of great significance in Scripture, we certainly recognize Jesus' supremacy (number 7).

Confronting the Truth

Christians who examine the Jewish views of Scripture must question the equal authority assigned to God's written law and the interpretations and commentaries later added by rabbis. The result is a body of teachings that are based on human traditions, which are constantly shifting, changing, and evolving. Can you imagine the uncertainty and anxiety in the lives of devout Jews? They attempt to follow the law, but they must also wonder whether they have chosen the correct set of authoritative ones.

Christianity is founded on God's Word. Our traditions, experiences, and scholarship stand under the authority of the Bible. While many Christian sects have misinterpreted Scripture and have taught wrong theology, the core essentials of Christianity, such as Christ's virgin birth, sinless life, vicarious death, bodily resurrection, provision of salvation by grace, and imminent return, have remained intact.

The sheer weight of attempting to obey the law causes the majority of Jews to abandon it altogether. Instead, they seek to follow the law symbolically by wearing the clothing or following the observances. The burden of the law can create a hunger for freedom in Christ.

" 'Don't assume that I came to destroy the Law or the Prophets. I did not come to destroy but to fulfill.' "
Matthew 5:17

" 'Come to Me, all of you who are weary and burdened, and I will give you rest. All of you, take up My yoke and learn from Me, because I am gentle and humble in heart, and you will find rest for yourselves. For My yoke is easy and My burden is light.' "
Matthew 11:28-30

Read Matthew 5:17 in the margin and check the correct statement.
○ **Jesus came to earth to destroy the law.**
○ **Jesus came to fulfill the law.**
○ **Jesus came to add to the law.**

Read Matthew 11:28-30 and check the correct statement.
○ **Jesus offers rest for those who are burdened.**
○ **Jesus' way is rewarding but exhausting.**
○ **Jesus' way is harder than the law of the old covenant.**

A Jew's abandonment of the law presents an opportunity for you to share that while human tradition is burdensome and the law is impossible to obey, Jesus came to fulfill that law (see Matt. 5:17) and to bring spiritual freedom (see Matt. 11:28-30).

Day 3: Why Am I Here? Purpose and Ethics

If the vast majority of Jewish adherents do not believe in any source of authority, on what do they base their lives? What is a Jew's purpose in life, and how does a Jew determine right and wrong? Again the answer resides in the sect with which the Jewish person is aligned. All Jewish sects believe in good works and ethics, but they vary in their approaches to these works and in the accountability they believe they will face.

All Jewish sects attempt to hold to the Ten Commandments (*Aseret ha-Dibrot*) as a guiding set of ethics. Furthermore, the concept of love and brotherhood supersedes adherence to the law. Many Christians view Jewish prospects as being stuck in a constricting system of laws and limitations. This is not the case for kabbalists, reconstructionists, or reformists. Although they may celebrate the holy days or observe the dietary laws, they are more concerned with social acts of charity and kindness.

For many Jews of this type, the driving ethical force beneath their actions is a desire to move from egoism to altruism. Regardless of how they interpret their actions, they believe that their purpose in life is to move from selfishness to charity. They work toward social justice, often investing themselves in feeding the poor and empowering the weak. Thus, they feel that they have fulfilled the greatest commandments. This is their Golden Rule (see Lev. 19:18). This is charity (*tzedakah*).

For orthodox Jews, however, the ethical standards and laws that guide every facet of life can be exacting. The Pentateuch (the first five books of the Bible) includes 613 unchangeable commandments (*mitzvot*). These commandments cover the entire range of life, from the foods they eat to the clothes they wear. Some laws tend to repeat one another or overlap, and the Jewish community has debated the interpretations.

However, all Jews consider the number of commandments significant. As Maimonides established 34 categories of the *mitzvot*, the complete list of the 613 became symbolic to Jews. Maimonides noted that there were 248 positive *mitzvot* ("You shall") and 365 negative *mitzvot* ("You shall not"). The first number coincides with the number of bones and organs in the human body, while the second number equates with the number of days in a solar calendar.

Some of the 613 *mitzvot* cannot be followed today. Because the Romans destroyed the temple in A.D. 70, keeping the temple laws is impossible. Jews no longer practice the sacrificial system with spotless animals and offerings. Instead, modern Jews substitute acts that symbolically fulfill the *mitzvot,* such as a special offering of money instead of the sacrifice of a dove.

Underline the correct phrase to complete each sentence.

> **Kabbalists, reconstructionists, and reformists place highest value
> on** (*charity and kindness, exacting obedience to standards*).
>
> **Orthodox Jews place highest value on** (*obedience to commandments,
> altruistic social involvement*).
>
> **All Jews believe in** (*good works and ethics, the same source of authority*).

All Jews emphasize good works and ethics. Kabbalists, reconstructionists, and reformists focus on charity and kindness. Orthodox Jews try to obey the commandments.

In addition to keeping the law, Orthodox Jews observe the sabbath, the seventh day of the week, as the day God rested from the work of creation (see Gen. 2:2-3). The sabbath begins at sundown on Friday and ends at sundown on Saturday. Synagogue and temple services are held on Friday evening.

Orthodox Jews observe holy days besides the sabbath. The Jewish New Year is *Rosh Hashanah*. The Day of Atonement (*Yom Kippur*), or the Day of Coverings, is the holiest day of the year. In ancient Israel it included the sacrifice of an animal to cover or atone for the sins of the people (see Lev. 16:1-34). *Purim* celebrates the deliverance of the Jews in Persia, as described in the Book of Esther. *Hanukkah*, celebrated in December, commemorates the victory of Judas Maccabees over the Syrians and the rededication of the temple in 164 B.C.

Festivals and feasts call Jews to remember God's goodness throughout their history. Passover (*Pesach*), recalling the exodus from Egypt, is the most important Jewish feast (see Lev. 23:4-14; Deut. 16:1-8). Pentecost (*Shavout*), or the Feast of Weeks, commemorates the giving of the law to Moses at Sinai. It is also associated with the wheat harvest (see Lev. 23:15-21; Deut. 16:9-12). The Feast of Tabernacles (*Succot*), or Booths, is associated with the fruit harvest in early fall (see Lev. 23:33-43; Deut. 16:13-17).

WITNESSING TIP

Become All Things

Learning more about Jewish customs and observances establishes common ground and enriches our Christian faith. The Jewish feasts and festivals recognized God's work in the lives of His people and foreshadowed the work of Christ. Be culturally sensitive when talking with Jews. Stress the Jewishness of faith in Jesus by using His Hebrew name, *Yeshua*, and by speaking of *Messiah* rather than *Christ*. Use *believer in the Messiah* instead of *Christian*. Use *the Messiah's return* instead of *Christ's second coming*. Avoid church words like *conversion* and *convert*. Use *congregation of believers* instead of *church* and *good news* instead of *gospel*.

Match the Jewish festival or holy day with the events it commemorates.

___ 1. *Yom Kippur*
___ 2. *Purim*
___ 3. *Hanukkah*
___ 4. Passover or *Pesach*
___ 5. Pentecost or *Shavout*
___ 6. Feast of Tabernacles or *Succot*

a. Fruit harvest
b. Deliverance of Jews in ancient Persia
c. Exodus from Egypt
d. Giving of the law to Moses
e. Day of Atonement, holiest day of the year
f. Rededication of the temple in 164 B.C.

You should have matched the Jewish festivals and holy days this way: 1. e, 2. b, 3. f, 4. c, 5. d, 6. a.

Confronting the Truth

As a college student, I learned an effective scriptural method of reaching Jews with the message of Christ's purpose for their lives. A large orthodox Jewish community lives near the Ohio State University campus. When my brothers and I were students, we could often make extra money by working for them on the sabbath (*shabbat*). Sometimes duties would consist of turning on lights or serving food. They strictly followed the dietary laws, known as the *kashrut* or kosher. The term does not simply apply to types of unclean foods, such as pork, but also to the preparation of the foods.

We took our lead from Paul's defense before Felix: " 'I always do my best to have a clear conscience toward God and men. After many years, I came to bring charitable gifts and offerings to my nation, and while I was doing this, some Jews from the province of Asia found me ritually purified in the temple' " (Acts 24:16-18). We would try to follow the kosher laws so that we could earn the right to speak to these Jews about Jesus. They were amused to see college students, especially since we were former Muslims, attempting to follow *kashrut*. Our desire not to be a stumbling block gave us opportunities to witness because the Jews warmed to us more readily than if we had simply been doing a job.

As a believer in Jesus Christ, Paul was free from the bondage of the vain attempts at following the law. Why would he submit to the requirements of the law this way?

Read 1 Corinthians 9:22 in the margin and check the reason Paul was willing to follow the law in this case.
○ **Paul denied Christ's complete fulfillment of the law on Calvary.**
○ **Paul felt that he was more holy than other Christians who did not follow the law.**
○ **Paul wanted to identify with those who followed the law in order to save them.**

"To the weak I became weak, in order to win the weak. I have become all things to all people, so that I may by all means save some."
1 Corinthians 9:22

Paul was willing to follow the law in order to reach those who still followed the law. Of course, we are free in Christ. However, I challenge you to consider the cost of a clear conscience before unbelieving people.

Check the things you would be willing to do to identify with Jews and gain an opportunity to share Christ's freedom.
○ **Subject yourself to their rules and regulations**
○ **Eat kosher foods even if they were foreign to you**
○ **Stop flaunting your freedom in front of them**
○ **Respect their traditions**
○ **Attend Jewish festivals and feasts**
○ **Visit a synagogue**

Think about the 613 commandments prescribed in the Old Testament. Do you believe it would be possible to follow all of them every single day? Neither do your Jewish friends. However, they may look on your teaching of grace as an escape route from obedience. Many orthodox Jews see the Christian concept of grace as a panacea that erases all responsibility. *I am forgiven*, they imagine us thinking, *so I can do what I want.* Instead, impress on your Jewish friends a Christian's responsibility to live by the Spirit of God, who is in our hearts.

In every instance Jesus did not obliterate the law but rather enriched and deepened it to reveal its true intent. The act of infidelity is wrong, Jesus taught, but so is lusting in our hearts (see Matt. 5:27-28). We must not hate our enemies but should pray for those who persecute us (see Matt. 5:43-44). Grace is not an escape; rather, it obligates us to live in obedience to our Lord. That includes sharing God's true purpose for Jewish people and for all people through a relationship with His Son.

Day 4: Where Am I Going? Eternity and Legacy

Do devout Jews believe in heaven and hell? Do they believe in a White Throne Judgment or a Bema Seat? Can a person be Jewish and still hold to reincarnation?

The answer is both yes and no. Yes, most Jews believe in some semblance of a biblical afterlife, both for the righteous and the wicked. Yes, some Jewish groups believe the good and the evil will be separated and will receive blessing or punishment. And yes, some modern forms of Judaism affirm an almost Hindu view of life cycles. In fact, Hasidic Jews have collections of reincarnation stories that trace back to the 19th century.[3] Hasidic Jews believe in the Jewish concept of *tikkun olam*, which means *repairing the universe*. Certain Jews, they purport, must return to earth in new bodies to pay the penalty for unforgiven sins they committed while on earth.

Yet most Orthodox Jews view eternity as a fulfillment of their messianic desire. The suffering of this present life will be atoned in the *Olam Ha-Ba*, the Messianic Age. The phrase, literally translated *the world to come*, is inspired by Old Testament imagery found in such books as Isaiah and Jeremiah. The beautiful descriptions found in these writings are viewed as a fulfillment of the Jewish hope for the nation: the Jewish people will return from exile to Israel, the Messiah will come, and peace will be restored.

Even the most progressive modern Jews anticipate some form of fulfillment of their hopes for Israel. They tend to view eternity as a corporate experience for the people of Israel instead of a time of individual accounting. Their works of social justice, they believe, will come to fruition when war ceases and humanity peacefully coexists. The Messiah will establish His reign and vindicate the Jewish people's suffering (see Isa. 2:2-5). In the Jewish concept of the afterlife, the entire world will recognize the God of Israel as the true God (see Mic. 4:2-3). Murder and strife will cease, and even sin itself will be impossible (see Zeph. 3:13). The temple, long ago destroyed, will be rebuilt, and thanksgiving sacrifices will be brought. The *Olam Ha-Ba* will be a time of abundance and joy.

Even those who interpret these events allegorically draw on this hope in the midst of present Jewish suffering. Such horrific events as the Holocaust are somewhat muted by the expectation of divine vindication and justice. Though the Jews as a people have suffered terribly, a day is coming when the injustice will be corrected.

Mark the following statements *T* (true) or *F* (false).

___ **1. All modern Jews share a common future expectation.**

___ **2. Modern Jews tend to view eternity as a corporate experience for the people of Israel.**

___ **3. Some Jews embrace a form of reincarnation.**

___ **4. Jews see no hope for future justice and divine vindication.**

The answers to the true/false statements are 1. F, 2. T, 3. T, 4. F.

Devout Jews do not view eternity only in corporate terms. Many Orthodox Jews point to such texts as Leviticus 26:3-9 as proof of individual blessing as well. The righteous hope to be reunited with their loved ones, and the wicked will be separated from the good. Disobeying God's commands brings about *kareit*, which means *being cut off from God and His people* (see Gen. 17:14). Many pious Jews see this eventuality as a spiritual separation from God for eternity. Therefore, some Jewish sects believe that the wicked will be annihilated; they simply cease to be. Others translate *Sheol as the grave of the wicked*, where the wicked will suffer eternally.

Orthodox Judaism holds to an intermittent state after death that is similar to the Roman Catholic concept of Purgatory. Many Jewish men and women refer to the place of spiritual reward as *Gan Eden*. Somewhat like the garden of Eden, it is a place of spiritual perfection. Conversely, the average person descends to a place of punishment or purification (*Gehinnom* or *She'ol*). One branch of the Hasidim teaches that every time a sin is committed, an angel of destruction is created. After we die, we are punished by the angels we created.

In many ways this view of punishment is like the biblical portrait of hell, but the marked distinction is that Orthodox Jews set a time limit in *Gehinnom*. The *Talmud* teaches that after a maximum period of 12 months the person is then allowed into *Olam Ha-Ba*. Only unrepentant souls are not allowed to ascend. Some sects believe those wicked are destroyed, while others hold to eternal damnation and suffering.

Confronting the Truth

Both Christianity and Judaism believe in eternal judgment and in the Messiah's rule as the righteous King who will sit on David's throne. Christians know that this Judge and Messiah is Jesus Christ. He is preparing a place of reward not for those who keep the law or do good but for those who accept His atonement (see John 14:2-3). Grace, God's unmerited and unearned favor toward sinners because of Christ's atonement, directly challenges the view that people must suffer for their own sins. The Messiah's kingdom will not be reserved for the Hebrew people but will consist of all the redeemed "from

Rely on Prayer

Prayer is particularly appropriate for the salvation of Jewish people. The Old Testament admonishes prayer for the spiritual well-being of the people of Israel (see Ps. 122:6-9), and one of the New Testament references to specific prayer for the lost. (Rom. 10:1) describes Paul's prayer for the salvation of the Jewish people.

every tribe and language and people and nation" (Rev. 5:9).

The Bible does not teach that punishment and reward are temporary or partial. Jesus' story in Luke 16:19-31 makes clear that a great chasm exists between heaven and hell that cannot be crossed. You can joyfully share with your Jewish friends that forgiveness through Christ is complete and permanent: "No condemnation now exists for those in Christ Jesus" (Rom. 8:1).

This assurance is foreign to Jews. Your certainty about your future destiny qualifies you to offer them hope in Christ. Some may be watching you from a distance and wondering: *Are the Christians as anxious about their future as we are? Do they worry about their eternal destination as much as we do?* Be ready to explain that you rest in the full salvation of the Lord.

Read the following Scriptures in your Bible. What does each one teach about a believer's ability to rest in Christ's full salvation?

John 10:27-30: _____

Ephesians 2:3-5: _____

Philippians 1:6: _____

When did you first or most powerfully realize the freedom of complete and permanent forgiveness?

_____

_____

Day 5: Is There Any Hope? Salvation and Security

Most modern and mainline Jews do not concern themselves with the concept of eternal salvation. Devout Jews, however, find salvation in a moral life, adherence to the law, and the ultimate anticipation of the *Moshiach* (Messiah). The belief in the advent of the *Moshiach* is fundamental to Orthodox Judaism. Three times a day Orthodox Jews repeat the *Shemoneh Esrei* prayer, which foresees the events that mark the coming of the Son of David:

- The ingathering of Jewish exiles from around the world
- The restoration of Jewish courts of justice
- The cessation of wickedness and sin
- The reward and honor of the righteous
- The rebuilding of Jerusalem as the eternal city of God
- The restoration of the line of King David
- The reinstatement of temple service

Orthodox Jews take an end-of-days view of salvation. The time of the *Moshiach*, called *Achareet Ha-Yameem* (*end of days*), is viewed as corporate salvation more than the salvation of the individual—Israel's salvation more than the Hebrew's salvation. The term *Moshiach* literally means *Anointed One*, but devout Jews do not see Him as a sacrifice or atonement but as a Ruler or King. Talmudic teachings about the Moshiach emphasize these features:

- He will be a descendant of King David (see Jer. 23:5). He is often referred to as "*Moshiach ben David*," accentuating His status as the son of David.
- He will be an expert in Jewish law and will be devout (see Isa. 11:2-5).
- He will be a great and righteous judge (see Jer. 33:15).
- He will be a human being, not a god or a demigod.

Interestingly, most Jewish scholars believe that humankind, not God, will set the date for the Messiah's coming. Variously, rabbis have taught that the *Moshiach* will come when He is needed most or when He is most deserved. Christians can readily see why Jews do not view Jesus Christ as the Messiah. The fulfillment for which devout Jews are looking did not take place in Jesus' first advent.

Jews today view Jesus in various ways. Some view Him as a myth, having never really existed. Some view Him as a great, respected teacher who understood Jewish law but no more. Still others view Him as one of many failed messiahs who attempted to reestablish David's throne. Some of those include Shimeon Bar Kochba, who led a revolt in Jerusalem in A.D. 135, and Shabbatai Tzvi, a Turkish Jew who attempted to lead a revolt in 1666 but instead converted to Islam. The Turks called him Dönmeh, which means *the convert*. Jews view him as an embarrassment and a failure. All of these men died without fulfilling their ultimate expectation.

> **WITNESSING TIP**
>
> ## Point to the Messiah
>
> Ask your Jewish friends to join you and other friends for a brief Bible study from the Jewish Bible, the Old Testament. Ask whether your friends would accept the gift of a New Testament. An edition that highlights the fulfillment of messianic prophecy would be ideal. If the opportunity arises, use Scriptures like the ones in the box on page 120 to show ways Jesus fulfilled messianic prophecy.

119

Read some of the Scriptures in "Jesus' Fulfillment of Messianic Prophecy" on this page and notice how Jesus fulfilled Jewish teachings about the Messiah.

_____

_____

Jesus' Fulfillment of Messianic Prophecy		
Prophecy	Verse(s)	Fulfillment
To be the Son of God	Psalm 2:7	John 3:16-17
To be born of the tribe of Judah	Genesis 49:10	Hebrews 7:14
To be born in Bethlehem	Micah 5:2	Matthew 2:1-6
To be a descendant of David	Isaiah 9:6-7	Luke 1:32-33
To die for the sins of His people	Isaiah 53:5-8	1 Corinthians 15:3-4
To die by crucifixion	Psalm 22:13-18	Luke 23:33
To sit at God's right hand	Psalm 110:1	Mark 16:19

Confronting the Truth

Reaching into the life of a devout Jew is difficult. Because Jews possess such a national and ethnic identity, conversion is equated with the rejection of their own people. Jewish families often have funeral services for their members who have come to Christ as Savior and Lord, where they are declared dead to them forever.

Consider the emotions of a Jewish person who considers accepting Christ. Check the attitudes a Christian witness needs to gain a hearing for the gospel.
○ **Caring**   ○ **Humble**   ○ **Angry**   ○ **Willing to listen**
○ **Thin-skinned** ○ **Inflexible**   ○ **Dogmatic**
○ **Patient**   ○ **Long-suffering** ○ **Demanding** ○ **Other:** _____

To reach a religious Jew, we must use Old Testament texts to reveal the true definition of salvation. Emphasize that Jesus Christ will in fact sit on the throne of David when He returns. He will in fact reestablish divine rule and justice. All of their messianic expectations will in fact be fulfilled when Jesus returns. Jerusalem will again become God's eternal and indivisible city.

However, devout Jews also anticipate the reestablishment of the sacrificial system. Why? To atone for their sins. They foresee a day when the Day of Atonement (*Yom Kippur*) will again be practiced. For a religion so consumed by national longing, orthodox Judaism certainly includes an emphasis on personal obligation and accountability. The vast majority of the 613 commandments address individual responsibility and accountability. Whether through obedience to the law or through acts of social benevolence, all Jews rely on works to earn personal salvation.

Just as the Messiah will meet the corporate needs of the nation of Israel, can He not also take care of the spiritual needs of the individual as well? Christians can use Old Testament references to eternal salvation to illustrate the salvation of the individual.

> *"I will give you a new heart and put a new spirit within you; I will remove your heart of stone and give you a heart of flesh."*
> Ezekiel 36:26

Read Ezekiel 36:26 in the margin. This verse addresses
○ **God's national rule**   ○ **God's promise of personal redemption.**

Verses like this record God's promise of a new and clean heart. This is more than just national rule. It is personal redemption.

A Christian witness can ask a Jewish seeker, "If personal redemption is also promised by God in the *Torah*, how will it come? Won't the *Moshiach* fulfill that promise as well? Isn't He capable of providing salvation as well as protection?" Explain that Christ's death is not a defeat but a messianic fulfillment. Use Isaiah 53 to show that the *Moshiach* provides both justice and mercy. He will rule with justice. He redeems by mercy (see 1 Pet. 2:24). His deliverance operates on both levels.

That was ultimately Paul's major point in responding to the Jews' accusations, in Acts 24:14-15. Of course Jesus rose from the dead. His physical and literal resurrection was necessary in order to return and fulfill the promise of His rule. If His resurrection was possible, so is His redemption.

Like the Apostle Paul, focus on the resurrection. Ask your Jewish friend this simple question: What one thing could the Jews have done to stop the movement and work of the apostles? What one thing could Jewish or Roman leaders have done to quell the schism within Judaism that followed Christ's resurrection? All they had to do was produce a body.

> *"... that Christ died for our sins according to the Scriptures, that He was buried, that He was raised on the third day according to the Scriptures, and that He appeared to Cephas [Peter], then to the Twelve. Then He appeared to over 500 brothers at one time."*
> 1 Corinthians 15:3-6

Read 1 Corinthians 15:3-6 in the margin. To whom did Jesus appear after His resurrection?

_____

Peter, James, John, and the others were loudly proclaiming Christ's resurrection. If the Jewish leaders knew where Joseph's tomb was and where Jesus was buried, all they had to do was dig up the body and display it for all to see. If the body was stolen and hidden, all they needed to do was have others testify that they saw the disciples moving the body or hiding the corpse. Yet they did not produce a single eyewitness or offer any counterproclamation. Did they also know that Jesus was alive?

Jesus' resurrection provided proof that Jesus was God in the flesh. He lived a sinless life, died on the cross, and rose again—all according to the Hebrew Scriptures. You have the privilege to share with Jews of all persuasions that salvation cannot be earned through works but is freely given as a gift from God to anyone who repents of sin and turns to God through faith in Jesus Christ.

Review this week's witnessing tips. Write in the margin one thing you will do to reach out to a Jewish person, develop a witnessing relationship with a Jew, or learn more about Judaism.

A Comparison of Beliefs

	Christianity	Judaism
God	One God who reveals Himself in three persons.	Absolutely one. Not triune.
Jesus	Unique Son of God who provided salvation through atoning death and resurrection.	Identity as Messiah rejected.
Source of Authority	Bible is divinely inspired and preserved and contains perfect instruction and truth.	The Hebrew Bible (Old Testament), which is inferior to tradition.
Humanity	Sinful by nature.	Basically good.
Sin	Sinful nature and choices are humanity's problem.	Sinful nature and the need for atonement are denied.
Salvation	Accepting God's gift of forgiveness through faith in Jesus Christ.	Earned through prayer and adherence to law or good deeds.

[1] Patricia Towle, "Hollywood Style of Kabbalah Is a Cult, Say Experts," *The Enquirer,* 14 June 2004 [cited 3 June 2005]. Available from the Internet: *www.rickross.com/reference/kabbalah/kabbalah72.html.*

[2] "What Is Reform Judaism?" Reform Judaism [cited 3 June 2005]. Available from the Internet: *www.rj.org/whatisrj.shtml.*

[3] These stories are called *Shivchei HaBesht.* One collection is Yonassan Gershom, *Jewish Tales of Reincarnation* (New York: Jason Aronson, 2000).

Viewer Guide
Group Session 6

Review Segment: Judaism

Judaism today is more _____ than a search for _____.

The best way to reach them is to be authentically _____.

When you reach them, the texts come _____.

All those rituals were given to point to the _____, not a replacement of Him.

The law can't _____, but it can show me I am _____.
The law can't make anyone _____, but the law restrains _____.

Teaching Segment: Islam: Medieval Mormonism

We know very little of the tragedy, the desperation, and the horror that take place in countries around the globe for Muslims who come to faith in _____ _____.

There are _____ mosques, study centers, training centers, and schools in America. There are virtually _____ Muslims in America that are accounted for.

Muslims believe in—
- The _____ _____
- Jesus' _____
- Jesus' _____

But Islam is not another form of _____.

Islam is a form of medieval _____. Muhammed took parts of the _____ he wanted, threw out parts he didn't want, and changed other parts. He turned Jesus into a _____ who looked to Islam's final prophet.

Many _____ sound like ours, but the definitions, characters, and names have changed substantially.

Everything is prescribed because of works. _____ is also a work.

Islam is not just a set of principles; it is _____ _____.

7 Islam

Medieval Mormonism

When we reached Jerusalem, the brothers welcomed us gladly. The following day Paul went in with us to James, and all the elders were present. After greeting them, he related one by one what God did among the Gentiles through his ministry.

When they heard it, they glorified God and said, "You see, brother, how many thousands of Jews there are who have believed, and they are all zealous for the law. But they have been told about you that you teach all the Jews who are among the Gentiles to abandon Moses, by telling them not to circumcise their children or to walk in our customs. So what is to be done? They will certainly hear that you've come. Therefore do what we tell you: We have four men who have obligated themselves with a vow. Take these men, purify yourself along with them, and pay for them to get their heads shaved. Then everyone will know that what they were told about you amounts to nothing, but that you yourself are also careful about observing the law. With regard to the Gentiles who have believed, we have written a letter containing our decision that they should keep themselves from food sacrificed to idols, from blood, from what is strangled, and from sexual immorality."

GLOBAL SNAPSHOT

- Muslims number about 1.7 billion worldwide.
- The various sects of Islam see themselves as the only true Muslims. Sunni do not recognize Shi'a as true Muslims.
- Muslims are the fastest-growing non-Christian group immigrating to America, almost double the next group, Hindus.

THIS WEEK'S GOAL

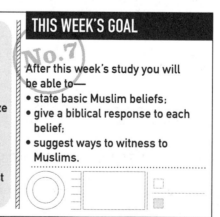

No.7

After this week's study you will be able to—

- state basic Muslim beliefs;
- give a biblical response to each belief;
- suggest ways to witness to Muslims.

Then the next day, Paul took the men, having purified himself along with them, and entered the temple, announcing the completion of the purification days when the offering for each of them would be made. As the seven days were about to end, the Jews from the province of Asia saw him in the temple complex, stirred up the whole crowd, and seized him, shouting, "Men of Israel, help! This is the man who teaches everyone everywhere against our people, our law, and this place. What's more, he also brought Greeks into the temple and has profaned this holy place." Acts 21:17-28

By Our Blood

Every year the Shi'a holiday of Ashura falls on the 10th day of Muharram, the first month on the Islamic calendar. This festival, commemorating a failure and a death, has no equivalent. An act of public mourning, it is as gruesome a display as the world has ever seen. Perhaps you have witnessed it on television.

Ashura marks the death of Hussein, the grandson of Muhammed, who had founded Islam. Hussein was killed in Karbala, in southern Iraq. His murderers were not infidel Jews or Christians. He was killed by other Muslims—Sunni Muslims—in A.D. 680. Shi'ite Muslims view Hussein as the victim of a political power play by the Sunni Muslims who had stolen the leadership of the movement and had usurped the Shi'ites' rightful place as the leaders of Islam. The Shi'a had wanted Muhammed's successor to be a blood heir. To quell their effort, the Sunni killed Hussein.

During Ashura hundreds of thousands of Shi'ites march down the streets of Karbala whipping themselves with chains and cutting their heads with machetes. This is not a symbolic display. They literally whip themselves. As blood pours down their faces, they lament their inability to protect their leader.

Ashura commemorates Hussein's murder, which split Islam into two main sects—Sunni and Shi'ite. However, it also illustrates Muhammed's practice of liberally borrowing from Christian teachings and history but changing them to fit his desires, just as Joseph Smith later adapted portions of the Bible to fit his message for Mormons. You see, for Muslims Ashura also commemorates the day Noah left the ark and the day God saved Moses from the Egyptians. Though there is no biblical evidence for such a celebration, Muslims use it to validate their religion.

The ritual observance of this holiday also illustrates the lengths to which Muslims go to find forgiveness, as well as the desperation of Islam. If ever a religion was dedicated to acts of obedience and ritualistic works, it is Islam. No religion combines the drive for world domination and a pursuit of salvation by righteous works as does Islam. Only medieval Roman Catholicism, with its Crusades and Inquisitions, has such a bloody history. Islam has been the driving antagonist of Christianity and Judaism since the Middle Ages.

Islam is more than a system of beliefs that governs spiritual exercises or worship services; Islam is a lifestyle. For Muslims (only Anglos refer to them as Moslems) every facet of life is dictated by protocols found in the Qur'an and in the *Hadith* (sayings of Muhammed). Everything is explicitly addressed by a dictum.

Because Islam is a nationalistic and exclusive religion, the ramifications of conversion to Christianity are stark. When I became a believer in Jesus Christ in 1982, my father—my hero in every sense of the word—disowned me. In one fleeting moment I lost my family, my home, my people, my culture, and my identity. Everything I had ever known as reality and existence collapsed. My church became my family. As far as my people were concerned, I became an infidel, worthy only of death. That threat has been issued numerous times since.

For my kinsmen, surrendering to Jesus as Lord is like signing your own death warrant. As you study this week, bear in mind the prison that confines your Muslim friends. Salvation for believers is a triumph of grace, but for them it carries the bittersweet by-product of rejection, renouncement, and even martyrdom.

Day 1: Who Am I? God and Humanity

Paul faced a unique problem. Having returned to Jerusalem from his missionary journey, Paul was warned by James that certain Jewish leaders were spreading the rumor that Paul was guilty of a serious crime: " 'telling them [the Jews] not to circumcise their children or to walk in our customs' " (Acts 21:21). The indictment against Paul was twofold: (1) he was accused of repudiating circumcision, which was explicitly commanded in the Old Testament, and (2) he was accused of repudiating the customs, which consisted of hundreds of additional laws that had developed over time.

Like first-century Judaism, Islam has an almost violent adherence to its laws and a bloody ethic. It is impossible to understand Islam without first knowing its history. Islam is the youngest world religion, founded in A.D. 610. The founder of Islam, Muhammed, was born at Saudi Arabia, the crossroads of commerce, in A.D. 570. As a merchant he sold his goods to the countless thousands of people who traveled the Middle Eastern trade routes. He lost his mother and father at an early age and was reared by his grandfather first and then an uncle. He was exposed to Coptic Christians, a cult that believed Jesus became God at some point of His earthly life, perhaps at His baptism. This erroneous teaching radically affected Muhammed's misunderstanding of Christianity.

On his 40th birthday Muhammed had a seizure. The *Hadith* begin with a description of his "rolling on the ground" and "roaring like a camel." When he came out of the seizure, he described to his wife, Khadijah, a vision. She convinced him his vision

WITNESSING TIP

Cultivate Relationships

When you approach Muslims, be very friendly and encourage them to talk first. Show genuine interest in their beliefs. Be familiar with Islamic beliefs and ask Muslims to show you passages from the Qur'an that you can examine together. Ask questions like: Will Islam guarantee the forgiveness of sins? Will it provide assurance of salvation? Be patient and do not argue. Otherwise, you may win the argument but lose a soul forever.

was from God. These visions, which continued for years, formed the basis for the Qur'an, the written holy book of Islam, and the beginning of a new religion.

Muhammed believed that Jews and Christians had changed God's teachings and had abandoned the truth altogether. He therefore considered them hell-bound and cultic. The core of his religion centered on his understanding of God. The name for the Islamic god is Allah. Muhammed taught that Allah has 99 names of terror and glory. Allah is beyond human understanding and approach. Muhammed's teaching about Allah's names is fundamental to understanding Islam.

The nature of Allah is called *tawhid*, meaning *absolute one*. This is more than monotheism (belief in one God); this is a rejection of the doctrine of the Trinity. The Holy Spirit in Islam is the angel Gibrael. No one—including Jesus—is called a son of God.

Check the statements that are true of Muhammed.
○ **1. He correctly understood the biblical teaching about Jesus' divinity.**
○ **2. He believed Jews and Christians had corrupted the faith and he must restore it.**
○ **3. He taught that God is personal and caring.**
○ **4. He accepted the doctrine of the Trinity.**
○ **5. He taught that the Holy Spirit is the angel Gibrael.**

You probably checked statements 2 and 5.

In spite of Muhammed's concept of God, some mainline Christian groups and missionary movements have recently taught that the Allah of the Qur'an and the God of the Bible are the same God. Let me be as clear as possible on this point: the Allah of Islam and the God of the Bible are not the same God. To say that they are shows a serious lack of knowledge of two major religions!

> *Muslims deny the fatherhood of God. Muslims deny the deity of the Son.*
> *Muslims deny the person of the Holy Spirit.*

Muslims believe that people do not inherit original sin from Adam and Eve. Adam and Eve were forgiven of their sin, so no sin remained in them. Thus, humans today, as their children, are not basically sinful. People are religious and long to worship Allah. Islam's central command is submission to Allah's will.

Humans commit sin because they are weak, fragile, and forgetful. Sin is breaking Allah's law and not doing His will. When a person commits sin, it harms him only. Sin does not grieve Allah. However, Allah, at His will, decides whom to punish and whom not to punish. People can increase their good deeds to gain Allah's favor and to earn forgiveness. The most serious sin committed is that of shirk, or considering Allah as more than one.

According to what you have read, what motivates Muslims?
○ **Honor** ○ **Freedom** ○ **Desire** ○ **Fear** ○ **Wisdom**

Read 2 Corinthians 5:14 in the margin. What compels Christians? _____

Fear motivates Muslims' decisions and actions because they have no assurance of favor with Allah. In contrast, Christians are driven by Christ's love.

Confronting the Truth

The sheer remoteness of Muslims from their god is shocking and heart-wrenching. It is impossible to put into words the abject fear this relationship involves. It's not the same as the biblical concept of fearing God.

Read Leviticus 19:14 in the margin. What do you think it means to fear God?

_____

"Christ's love compels us, since we have reached this conclusion: if One died for all, then all died."
2 Corinthians 5:14

" 'Fear your God; I am the Lord.' "
Leviticus 19:14

When the Bible speaks of the fear of God, it refers to our absolute reverence. When Muslims fear Allah, they mean that they are afraid. Muslims' fear of direct, immediate, and eternal reprisal drives virtually every deed.

Do you remember how you felt the moment you realized that you were outside God's grace? Imagine experiencing that desperate feeling every day of your life, even as you carry out your rituals and prayers. This is life without grace, a life of abject fear.

Islam views people as being born without sin but capable of breaking Allah's law. To make it into heaven, they must do more good than bad, think more good than bad, and be more good than bad. They must be 51 percent righteous at the time of death to make it into paradise.

Unlike Muslims, Christians aren't terrified by God, because we believe that He is knowable and personal. God is one, but He has revealed Himself in the plural form Elohim (see Gen. 1:26). The Bible clearly reveals that God's oneness comprises three persons—Father, Son, and Holy Spirit (see Matt. 28:19). God's triune nature is part of His mystery and greatness.

How does God's revelation to you as Father, Son, and Holy Spirit help you know Him more deeply and intimately?

Father: _____

Son: _____

Holy Spirit: _____

God's triune nature helps us understand Him as truly personal and capable of expressing His nature in a variety of ways. God's work in accomplishing salvation is through the person of Jesus Christ.

Christians do not accept Islam's teachings on humanity and sin. Christians believe that people are made in God's image (see Gen. 1:27), but because they inherit a sinful nature, all commit sin (see Rom. 3:23; 5:12,19). The Bible teaches that sin is not error but missing the mark of God's standard. People miss God's mark by rebelling against Him (see Ps. 51:4) and by breaking the law (see 1 John 3:4). All people have sinned and are guilty before God (see Rom. 3:23).

Human sin grieves God (see Ps. 78:40). It breaks fellowship between the person and God and with others (see Isa. 59:2-3; 1 John 1:3,6-7). The Bible teaches that God hates sin but loves the sinner (see Rom. 5:6-8) and forgives the sins of all who repent and trust in Jesus (see 2 Cor. 5:19-21).

Mark each teaching on humanity and sin either *I* for *Islam* or *C* for *Christian*.
___ 1. **People are born with a sinful nature.**
___ 2. **People are born pure.**
___ 3. **Sin is error resulting from weakness.**
___ 4. **Sin is missing God's standard.**
___ 5. **Sin breaks fellowship with the deity.**
___ 6. **There is no relationship with the deity.**
___ 7. **The deity forgives sin.**
___ 8. **The deity punishes sinners according to His will.**

Christianity differs from Islam in the conviction that good works do not earn forgiveness, which is a free gift of God's grace (see Eph. 2:8-9). Assurance of our status before God doesn't depend on being 51 percent good through our own efforts but on being 100 percent saved by faith in Jesus Christ's atonement.

The Christian beliefs about humanity and sin are expressed in numbers 1, 4, 5, and 7.

Day 2: How Can I Know? Authority and Truth

From Muhammed's 40th birthday in 610 until his death in 632, he vehemently preached the Islamic religion. However, it was not until the final 10 years of his life (July 622) that Islam became a force with which to be reckoned. The warring tribes into which Muhammed was born had to unite against a common enemy to stop their endless territorial skirmishes. At one point Muhammed was chased out of Mecca and fled to Medina. However, when he returned, he had an army of believers.

The central message he preached? The Jews had Allah's message but corrupted it. The Christians had the truth but abandoned it. Now Muhammed was the final messenger, and he was preaching the truth: Allah had called him to preach Islam, and it would conquer the world.

To justify his message, Muhammed needed an authority greater than his own word. This authority, known as the Qur'an, was composed of the "revelations" he directly received from Allah and recorded. As a record of Allah's exact words, the Qur'an is believed to completely reveal His will. It is the source of the individual's faith and practice, as well as a guide to society. The Qur'an looks imposing but is actually shorter than any sacred book among the world religions. Its 114 chapters consist of approximately 6,000 verses. Yet within its covers we find the source of all Islamic doctrine.

The Sacred Book Mistaken

Muhammed's handling of Scripture in the 7th century is much like that of Mormon leaders Joseph Smith and Brigham Young in the 19th century. Both Mormonism and Islam borrowed parts of the Bible they liked, discarded or changed others, turned Jesus into a prophet, consigned women to an eternity of sexual slavery, and made salvation entirely works-related. Thus, as this week's title affirms, Islam might be thought of as a type of medieval Mormonism.

Many Christians are surprised to discover that the Qur'an includes parts of the Old Testament, such as the first five books of the Bible. However, the accounts have been modified. Although the Qur'an contains many references to the *Torah,* the psalms of David, and the four Gospels, the Qur'an emphatically claims to be the final source of

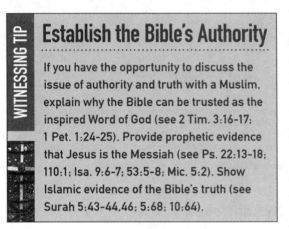

WITNESSING TIP

Establish the Bible's Authority

If you have the opportunity to discuss the issue of authority and truth with a Muslim, explain why the Bible can be trusted as the inspired Word of God (see 2 Tim. 3:16-17; 1 Pet. 1:24-25). Provide prophetic evidence that Jesus is the Messiah (see Ps. 22:13-18; 110:1; Isa. 9:6-7; 53:5-8; Mic. 5:2). Show Islamic evidence of the Bible's truth (see Surah 5:43-44,46; 5:68; 10:64).

authority: "You People of the Book [Jews and Christians]! Why do you clothe truth with falsehood and conceal the truth, while you have knowledge? ... There is among them a section who distort the Book with their tongues: you would think it is part of the Book, but it is no part of the Book" (Surah 3:71,78).

The Sacred Book Mended

When Muhammed was convinced that his visions were from Allah, he had another problem: he was illiterate. Therefore, he used scribes to write down his words. The collection of his visions became the Qur'an, which Muslims consider the actual recorded words of Allah, as if one continuous speech.

As Allah's final and unchangeable revelation, the Qur'an is the source and proof of Islam: "This is the Book; in it is guidance sure, without doubt, to those who fear Allah; who believe in the Unseen ... and who believe in the Revelation sent to you ... (in their hearts) have the assurance of the Hereafter" (Surah 1:2-4).

The Qur'an is intended to be understood and read in Arabic. Therefore, Muslims consider it a religious obligation to learn, read, and recite the Qur'an in Arabic. The Qur'an says of itself: "No changes can there be in the Words of Allah. This is indeed the supreme Triumph" (Surah 10:64). Allah guards the Qur'an from any distortion or alteration (see Surah 15:9).

Check the statements that Muslims believe about the Qur'an.
○ 1. It contains revelations received directly from Allah.
○ 2. It is the actual words of Allah, as if one continuous speech.
○ 3. It is divinely inspired and recorded by many authors.
○ 4. Allah has protected it from any changes.

Statements 1, 2, and 4 should be checked.

The Sacred Text Misunderstood

The Qur'an includes a number of biblical stories that it misunderstands or blatantly changes. For example, the Qur'an misinterprets the Christian belief in the Trinity to mean God the Father; His wife, Mary; and their Son, Jesus (see Surah 5:116).

The most important example of revising the biblical text has serious implications. In Surah 27:100-111 the Qur'an tells the story of Abraham's taking his son to the top of the mountain to sacrifice him. At the last minute Allah provides a substitute and spares the life of ... Ishmael. Allow that to sink in for a moment. Muhammed changed the biblical story to relate that instead of Isaac, Ishmael was being sacrificed. If Ishmael were being sacrificed on Mount Moriah, then the land—including Jerusalem—rightly belongs to his descendants. Muslims believe that they are Ishmael's descendants. Therefore, Muslims believe they have the rights to the land, not the Jews.

Confronting the Truth

Christians do not believe that the Qur'an is a divinely revealed book, because it contains contradictory messages. For example, the Qur'an accepts Jesus' sinless birth while rejecting His divinity and death on the cross. Christians believe that the Bible is the perfect record of God's revelation of Himself to humanity. Because the Scriptures are divinely inspired and preserved, they are completely true and trustworthy (see 2 Tim. 3:16-17; 1 Pet. 1:25; 2 Pet. 1:19-21).

For which reason do you believe that the Bible is God's inspired Word?
○ **Purely by faith**
○ **By faith in credible evidence**
○ **Primarily because of the evidence in Scripture**
○ **Other:** _____

Explain your answer. _____

_____

Muslims must accept the Qur'an completely by faith, in spite of its contradictions. This area of written authority is one of the most difficult areas to discuss with Muslims. Regardless of the biblical text you cite, they simply respond that the Qur'an corrects the mistakes in the Bible. Yet a few questions arise from the Muslim view of authority.

If the Qur'an can be understood only in Arabic and only 20 percent of Muslims worldwide understand and speak Arabic, does that mean 80 percent of the Muslim world cannot understand Islam? Similarly, if the Qur'an is perfect, why do so many devout Muslims disagree on the fundamentals of the religion? Sunni and Shi'ite Muslims disagree on even the path to heaven. Which group is correct? Christians differ on some points, but all evangelicals agree on the absolutes of the faith.

If you had been taught all your life to unquestioningly believe the Qur'an, which of the questions above would most open your mind? Why?

_____

Pray that God will tear down the wall of fear and misinformation that keeps the Muslims you know from seeing the truth about the Qur'an and the Bible.

Day 3: Why Am I Here? Purpose and Ethics

Early in the morning, from minarets (towers of Islamic mosques) around the world, a single voice calls all Muslims to prayer. Rising with a fervent cry, the voice resonates in Arabic, *"Allah Hu Akbar! Allah Hu Akbar!"* The words translate, "Allah is great! Allah is the greatest!" The cry itself is a signal. Muslims begin their day with prayer, the first of five regulated prayer times. Facing Mecca, Muslims stand, kneel, and bow on their prayer rugs. It is part and parcel of a Muslim's daily life.

While we will deal with the road to Islamic salvation later this week, it is impossible to separate the ethics of Islam from its doctrines. Islam is a way of life, and each life must be lived in such a way as to achieve salvation.

Enter *jihad*. It means *warfare*. Though there has been much discussion about the term, and we have seen its gruesome effects, *jihad* actually has two dimensions: personal and corporate. It comprises the ethical system and purpose of Islamic life.

WITNESSING TIP

Demonstrate Christian Love

Believers are challenged by the spread of Islam, but we are not at war with Muslims. Our attitude must be love and acceptance, because God accepts and loves people as they are and wants them to enter a relationship with Him (see 2 Pet. 3:9). Against love there is no defense. Therefore, be sure that the love of Christ is your motive in reaching Muslims with the gospel (see John 3:16; Acts 17). Ministry is an excellent way to express the love of Jesus.

Personal Jihad:
Warfare Against the Flesh

All Muslims are called to fight against their earthly, sinful desires. This warfare is personal *jihad*. Muslims believe that each person is pure-born—born without sin. However, sin quickly enters the picture through personal choice. Shirk, which is considering Allah as

132

more than one, is the Arabic equivalent of the Roman Catholic doctrine of mortal sin—sin that cannot be forgiven.

To wage war against sin, Muslims must follow the prescriptions of Islam as closely as possible. They strive to follow the examples of the many heroes of the religion, who have been revised from biblical history to fit Islam. Consider Abraham (called Ibrahim in Arabic): "No, Abraham was neither a Jew nor a Nazarene. He was of pure faith, a Muslim. He was never of the idolaters. Surely, the people who are nearest to Abraham are those who followed him, and this Prophet [Muhammed], and those who believe. Allah is the Guardian of the believers" (Surah 3:67-71). Abraham was supposedly a practicing Muslim 2,700 years before Muhammed even crafted the Islamic faith.

Islamic laws affect all areas of Muslim life. Foods are divided into *halal* (lawful), *haram* (forbidden), and *mushbooh* (questionable). Dress is to be modest, with men avoiding gold-colored clothing and women wearing the veil (*hijab*). A man is allowed to have up to four wives, but he must provide for them. He is allowed to beat them as a last resort (see Surah 4:34).

Match the concepts with their descriptions.

___ **1. *Jihad***   **a. The veil**
___ **2. Shirk**   **b. Believing Allah is more than one**
___ **3. *Hijab***   **c. Personal and corporate warfare**

Muslims must also follow the Five Pillars of Islam; observe Ramadan and the feasts (called *eid*s); and faithfully attend the mosque (*masjid*), especially on Friday (*jumiat*). Although some Western Muslims reject some of the protocols of Islam, they are in the minority. For instance, if you visited my country, Turkey, you would see many Muslim women walking the streets of Istanbul without the veil. However, a trip to Ankara would quickly show you that Istanbul is the exception, not the rule.

The correct answers are 1. c, 2. b, 3. a.

Because Muhammed was exposed to Roman Catholicism and Coptic Christianity, he incorporated many of their practices into Islam. Just as Roman Catholics use the rosary in their prayer lives, Muslims use beads called *mesbah* to count the 99 names of Allah in prayer. Roman Catholics fast during the season of Lent; Muslims fast during the month of Ramadan. Roman Catholics make pilgrimages to Jerusalem; Muslims must make *hajj*, a pilgrimage to Mecca, once during their lives.

The Five Pillars of Islam

1. **Kalima.** The confession "There is no god but Allah. Muhammed is the messenger of Allah."
2. **Salat.** Prayer five times daily facing Mecca
3. **Zakat.** Almsgiving of 1/40 of income
4. **Sawm.** Fasting during the month of Ramadan
5. **Hajj.** The pilgrimage to Mecca, made once in a lifetime

Write a key word that summarizes each of the Five Pillars of Islam.

1. _____

2. _____

3. _____

4. _____

5. _____

A Peaceful Religion?

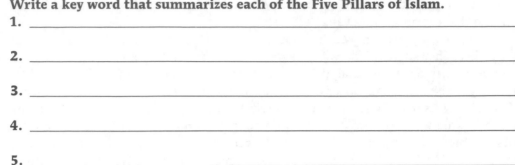

Airliners flown into buildings, ritualistic beheadings broadcast on Arabic television, calls for continued *jihad*—these come only from extremist fundamentalists, say many Muslim leaders who insist Islam is a peaceful religion. Yet a password-protected Arabic Web site has about 40 different discussion threads berating individual Christians, making threatening statements about them, posting pictures and address information on them, or seeking information with the hopes of tracking them down.[1]

Corporate Jihad:
Warfare Against the Infidel

The more notorious definition of *jihad* is corporate *jihad*—warfare against infidels (*akafir*). We see the awful images of women being killed by their own family members in honor killings. We see Christians slaughtered. Corporate *jihad* is a central tenet of Islam, regardless of what modern redactors say.

Jihad on a national or global scale originates from the Islamic doctrine of *sharia* law. The doctrine of Islamic theocracy, *sharia* law declares that Muslim leaders (*imams* and *ayatollahs*) rule the country. The laws of Islamic republics are composed of the teachings of the Qur'an (the words of Allah) and their interpretation of the *Hadith* (the words, examples, and teachings of Muhammed). Dictating punishment for the Muslims who live in those countries, Islamic laws are roughly equivalent to an eye-for-an-eye form of justice.

Sharia law also affects non-Muslims living in Islamic republics. Non-Muslims must pay a tax (*jizyat*) to live in the country. Christians may not build or remodel churches and are forbidden to evangelize. A Christian cannot forbid his child from marrying a Muslim and converting to Islam, but a Muslim child may not marry a Christian and convert to Christianity.

Islam teaches that this warfare must be waged from a defensive posture. Muslims are commanded to fight against the infidels when Islam is threatened. Muslims also believe that Allah will end the world when all countries of the earth are ruled by Islam. For them, therefore, this warfare is part of prophecy.

There is little substantiation for the position that Islam is a religion of peace. In 1,300 years Islam has never peacefully coexisted with other faiths in any country where the Muslim population was in the majority. Even though Turkey is used as an example of this peaceful coexistence, churches throughout the country are routinely closed or burned.

Complete the following sentences and check your answers against the previous paragraphs.

Corporate _____ is a central tenet of Islam.

Under *sharia* law the Muslim leaders _____ the country.

Under *sharia* law Christians are forbidden from _____ and building

_____, and they must pay a special _____ called *jizyat*.

Muslims are commanded to fight against the _____.

Modern spin doctors would have quite a problem refuting the Qur'an's many citations calling for *jihad* against infidels.

In the following sections from the Qur'an, underline words and phrases that command violent acts of *jihad*.

> *Fight those who believe not in Allah nor the Last Day, nor hold that forbidden which has been forbidden by Allah and His Messenger, nor acknowledge the Religion of Truth, from among the People of the Book [Jews and Christians], until they pay compensation with willing submission, and feel themselves subdued (Surah 9:29).*

> *Strongest among men in enmity to the Believers (Muslims) will you find the Jews and Pagans (Surah 5:82).*

> *Those who disbelieve, among the People of the Book and among the Polytheists, will be in hell-fire, to dwell therein (for aye). They are the worst of creatures (Surah 98:6).*

> *When the forbidden months are past, then fight and slay the pagans wherever you find them, and seize them, beleaguer them, and lie in wait for them, in every stratagem of war (Surah 9:5)*

Personal and corporate *jihad* merge when individual Muslims are promised immediate salvation if they fight in corporate *jihad*. For example, suicide bombers are promised virgins in paradise for their actions. Many Muslim apologists claim that the Qur'an does not teach such things.

Confronting the Truth

How does a Christian respond to Muslims who argue that they do not believe in *jihad* as holy war? Simply believe them. Most Muslims in this country have accepted the Western way of life, embracing democracy, a free-market economy, and religious liberty. I regularly meet Muslims who are embarrassed by the acts of Muslim *jihadin* who bomb and kill non-Muslims.

Two questions are at stake here. One is, Is Islam peaceful? Tragically, history records that the answer is no. However, the history of Christianity is also marked by many acts of violence against non-Christians. Even if the acts were perpetrated by people who were decidedly different from present-day evangelicals, the Muslim world does not understand this difference. They see these past acts as a form of Christian *jihad*.

The second question, however, is quite different: Are there peaceful Muslims? The answer is yes. They are caught in the crosshairs of a dilemma. On the one hand, they are mortified by the acts of Wahabi Muslims and terrorists. On the other hand, they are viewed as backslidden by the rest of the Muslim world. For Muslims who depend on personal or corporate *jihad* for salvation and assurance, you can offer true purpose in life through a relationship with Jesus Christ.

Time for an attitude check. Read the Culture Clash on page 134 and answer these questions.

Has terrorist violence against America affected your ability to love Muslims the way Jesus does?   ○ **Yes**   ○ **No**
Would you be willing to put aside any hatred you harbor toward Muslims?
○ **Yes**   ○ **No**

Stop and pray about your responses. If you can't love Muslims, talk with God about this. Ask Him to help you love and reach out to Muslims.

Day 4: Where Am I Going? Eternity and Legacy

Eternity for a Muslim is a discomfiting question. Islam clearly teaches that judgment awaits every living being, and this judgment is based on the person's works while here on earth: "Every soul shall have a taste of death: and only on the Day of Judgment shall you be paid for your full recompense. Only he who is saved far from the Fire and admitted to the Garden will have succeeded: For the life of this world is but goods and chattels of deception" (Surah 3:185).

DEFINITION

Wahabism (Wahhabism)

A very strict, purist, fundamentalist form of Islam, deviating specifically from Sunni Islam. It advocates a very legalistic understanding and practice in matters of faith or religion and takes the entire Qur'an quite literally. Wahabism seeks to remove what it perceives as innovations, superstitions, or heresies from Islam, thus seeing itself as a reformer or, more precisely, a restorer of Islam. In recent years it has become a dominant form of Islam through proselytization.[2]

Interestingly, the inauguration of eternal judgment in Islam is the coming of Jesus. Although Muslims view Jesus as only a prophet of Allah, the Qur'an teaches that Jesus never died. Muslims believe that God took Jesus from the cross and substituted Judas or someone who looked like Jesus. Jesus was then taken to heaven, where He is alive and will return to declare Allah's judgment (see Surah 19:33). Borrowing a theme from Christianity, Islam teaches that a scroll will be read at judgment, and each person will have to read the account of his or her actions.

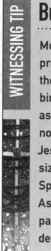

WITNESSING TIP

Build on Respect for Jesus

Muslims have great respect for Jesus as a prophet of God. He is mentioned 97 times in the Qur'an, which affirms His supernatural birth, life of miracles, compassion, and ascension to heaven. However, Muslims do not accept Jesus as the Son of God. Explain Jesus' eternal nature and sonship, emphasizing that He was conceived by the Holy Spirit without physical relations with Mary. As God in the flesh, He died on the cross to pay for humanity's sin and rose from the dead in power and victory.

Complete the following as a faithful Muslim would. Check your answers against the previous paragraphs.

Judgment is based on _____ .

The coming of Jesus begins _____ .

A scroll will be read at judgment describing _____ .

The judgment of non-Muslims is quite harsh. Muhammed taught that the punishment exacted on earth against unbelievers is simply a harbinger of the coming punishment of hell: "The punishment of those who wage war against Allah and His Messenger, and strive with might and main for mischief through the land is: execution, or crucifixion, or the cutting off of hands, and feet from opposite sides, or exile from the land: That is their disgrace in this world, and a heavy punishment is theirs in the Hereafter" (Surah 5:33). The fourth chapter of the Qur'an also adds, "Those who reject our Signs. We shall soon cast into the Fire: As often as their skins are roasted through, we shall change them for fresh skins, that they may taste the Chastisement: for Allah is Exalted in Power, Wise" (Surah 4:56).

Likewise, the judgment for devout Muslims is described in vivid imagery: "Those who believe and do deeds of righteousness, we shall soon admit to Gardens, with rivers flowing beneath, their eternal home" (Surah 4:57).

Life on earth is a mere dress rehearsal for eternity. Unlike Hinduism and Buddhism, Islam offers no hope of reincarnation. By performing good deeds and obeying the Five Pillars and the Qur'an, Muslims hope to be good enough to enter paradise.

Confronting the Truth

You can use the Muslim belief that Jesus will return to declare judgment as a launching pad for dialogue. Ask a Muslim who speaks of this judgment and the scrolls, "Will Jesus have to make an account?" If he says yes, you can continue: "Who is the greater prophet, Jesus or Muhammed? Will Muhammed have to make an account as well?

This is a good discussion point because Muhammed questioned his own eternal destiny! As recorded in Bukhari's *Hadith*, Muhammed made this astonishing admission while speaking with a widow. She comforted herself with the thought that her beloved husband was in paradise. However, Muhammed questioned her assurance: " 'How do you know that Allah has honored him?' [She] replied, 'I do not know. May my father and my mother be sacrificed for you, O Allah's Apostle! But who else is worthy of it (if not 'Uthman)?' He said, 'As to him, by Allah, death has overtaken him, and I hope the best for him. By Allah, though I am the Apostle of Allah, yet I do not know what Allah will do to me' " (Bukhari 5.266). If the founder of the religion does not have assurance of his eternity, how can the average Muslim?

Read John 14:2-3 and 1 John 2:24-25 in the margin. What does the biblical teaching on eternal security mean to you personally?

_____

Can you now see how liberating grace is? Because of Christ's atonement on the cross of Calvary, Muslims do not have to rely on their works or question their destiny. Those who accept Christ as Savior and Lord have assurance of salvation and the hope of personal fellowship with God for eternity. It is not their salvation; it is His. He purchased their eternal security with His blood.

Day 5: Is There Any Hope? Salvation and Security

Salvation for Muslims is ultimately based on the fundamental creed in Islam: "*Ilaha illa Allah. Muhammed rasul Allah,*" which is translated, "There is no god but Allah. Muhammed is the messenger of Allah." This confession, called the *kalima*, is the first step in becoming a Muslim. At any point in life someone can recite these words and instantaneously become a Muslim, as long as they are sincere.

However, Islam teaches that every person on earth is born a Muslim. When an adherent of another religion becomes a Muslim, it is called reversion, not conversion, because the person is perceived as coming back to the religion of their infancy. Following this confession, an individual must follow four other essential disciplines of salvation prescribed by the Five Pillars of Islam:

- *Salat*: prayer five times daily facing Mecca
- *Zakat*: almsgiving of ¹⁄₄₀ of income
- *Sawm*: fasting during the month of Ramadan
- *Hajj*: the pilgrimage to Mecca, made once in a lifetime

" 'In My Father's house are many dwelling places; if not, I would have told you. I am going away to prepare a place for you. If I go away and prepare a place for you, I will come back and receive you to Myself, so that where I am you may be also.' "
John 14:2-3

"What you have heard from the beginning must remain in you. If what you have heard from the beginning remains in you, then you will remain in the Son and in the Father. And this is the promise that He Himself made to us: eternal life."
1 John 2:24-25

138

Five times a day, as prescribed by the lunar or solar calendar (Muslims can't even agree on the calendar), Muslims follow the same actions that have been observed for 1,300 years: First, they perform *wudu* (ablution), washing their hands, head, and feet and cleaning out their nostrils. Then they enter the prayer room, if in the mosque, or approach their prayer rug, facing Mecca. Males stand closest to Mecca and line up in rows according to age, from the eldest men to the youngest boys. Separated by a gap, women and girls form their rows. The prayer positions are strictly prescribed, following one complete revolution that moves from standing to bowing, to standing again, to kneeling, to placing their foreheads on the ground, then kneeling again.

The prayers themselves are strictly prescribed. Muslims repeat the first surah (chapter) of the Qur'an over and over. The prescribed prayers point to a fundamental doctrine called a foundation in Islam: absolute sovereignty and predestination (*kismet*). Orthodox Islam teaches that if you break your arm, you are to say "*En sh'Allah*," meaning "Allah wills it." Muslims say this phrase countless times each day.

How does Islam's five-times-a-day prayer routine differ from your prayer life?

How can anyone possibly keep all of Allah's laws? No one can. Even though Muslims deny that people inherit a sinful nature, they understand that people sin because of weakness or error. These sins work against the faithful Muslim's good works. When considering the Muslim concept of salvation, keep this reality in mind: *Muslims live and die by scales. They must do more good than bad to make it into heaven.*

The enormity of the scales looms over Muslims' heads like the sword of Damocles, poised and ready to cut them down at any moment. All of Muhammed's doctrinal choices contributed to the concept of judgment by scales. Why did he reject the idea of original sin? Because if we inherited our sin nature from the first Adam, the work of the final Adam (Jesus) is important. Why deny Christ's crucifixion? Because if He actually shed His blood for a purpose, our blood is irrelevant.

Unlike other world religions that do not directly mention Jesus, the Qur'an contains numerous references to Jesus. Called *Isa* in Arabic, He is held in high esteem in Islam. However, like all others who want to respect an image of Jesus that robs Him of His divinity, Islam's respect falls tragically short. Islam views Jesus as one of thousands of special messengers of Allah sent to guide people away from infidelity, idolatry, and superstition. Unlike Jesus, who was sent only to the Jews, Muhammed was sent to all people; he is the last prophet of Allah.

The reason Islam denies Christ's death, burial, and resurrection is simple: if Jesus Christ died, He was either a failure or the Redeemer. Because Islam wants to respect Jesus, the former alternative is impossible. Because Islam believes that people must atone for their own sins, it also denies that Jesus is the Redeemer. Muslims do not deny blood atonement, but it is human blood they depend on.

Show Sensitivity

Be aware that many Muslims believe that all Americans are Christians. Because American society is immoral, they believe that all Christians are immoral. Your Christlike lifestyle can prove otherwise. State your belief in high moral standards. Be sensitive to Muslim cultural teachings. For example, a Muslim man may resist a witness from a woman. Muslims may be uncomfortable attending a Bible study if pictures of Jesus are on the walls.

Confronting the Truth

The Bible affirms that Jesus is much more than a prophet. He was supernaturally conceived by the Holy Spirit and was born of the virgin Mary. Jesus was God's unique Son. During His earthly ministry He carried out His Father's will. He died on a cross as the sacrifice for the sins of the world, was raised from the dead, and is exalted at the right hand of the Father in heaven. Jesus provides salvation for all who repent of their sins and confess Him as Lord. Because His blood atoned for sin, salvation is a gift of grace through faith in Jesus Christ (see Eph. 2:8-10). Contrary to Muslim practice, it is impossible to earn salvation by good works or by religious deeds and exercises.

Read the following Scriptures in your Bible. Paraphrase them in words you could use to explain to a Muslim the futility of works salvation. You may need to read the context to adequately explain the verses.

Matthew 7:22-23: _____

Romans 9:32: _____

Galatians 2:16: _____

Titus 3:1-7: _____

If you talk with Muslims about Jesus, they may say something like this: "Show me one place in the Bible where Jesus claims to be God. How can He pray to His Father if He is part of the Father?" Immediately a believer is drawn to John 8:50-58. When Jesus was cornered by the Jews and their leaders, they asked how He knew Abraham. Jesus answered, " 'Before Abraham was, I AM.' " By using the one unspeakable name that God used when He spoke to Moses (see Ex. 3:14), Jesus claimed to be God. The Jews picked up rocks to stone Him for blasphemy.

Even though the Qur'an teaches that Jesus was not crucified, it does teach that He was indicted for blasphemy (see Surah 4:157-159). Could Jesus be a prophet in Islam if He lied? If Jesus claimed to be God, could He be one of the prophets of Islam?

Jesus' blood is another theme you can use to connect with Muslims. If Jesus was crucified, His blood was either for a purpose or a tragedy. In Islam sin is not paid for; it is weighed. How can a just God throw away sin without any punishment? Grace is truly an act of absolute payment. On the cross of Calvary Jesus took God's wrath against all sin. In one eternal moment Jesus became sin. This is grace. And it is grace that Muslims so desperately need.

Read the witnessing tip on page 140. Why are a Christian's behavior and attitude so important in seeking to share Christ with a Muslim (or anyone)?

A Comparison of Beliefs

	Christianity	Islam
God	One triune God who is personal and knowable.	Allah is absolutely one. Not triune. Not personal.
Jesus	Unique Son of God who provided salvation through atoning death and resurrection.	Prophet. Not God's Son.
Source of Authority	Bible is divinely inspired and preserved and contains perfect instruction and truth.	The Qur'an is Allah's exact words.
Humanity	Made in God's image but sinful by nature.	No sinful nature. Born pure. Basically religious.
Sin	Sinful nature and choices are humanity's problem.	Breaking Allah's law and not doing His will are sin.
Salvation	Accepting God's gift of forgiveness through faith in Jesus Christ.	Based on Allah's will. Pursued by conforming to Five Pillars.

[1]Daveed Gartenstein-Ross, "U.S. Muslims Stalk More Infidels," 7 February 2005 [cited 2 May 2005]. Available from the Internet: *www.frontpagemag.com/Articles/ReadArticle.asp?ID=16879.*
[2]*http://en.wikipedia.org/wiki/Wahhabism.*

Viewer Guide

Group Session 7

Review Segment: Islam

Thousands of conditional _____, _____, and prescribed _____ are given to the Muslim.

There is no such thing as an _____ covenant in Islam.

There is no other system on the planet as _____-oriented as Islam. _____ is perceived as giving the works.

You hope to make it into paradise if you've got more _____ than _____ works. Paradise is measured by one hundred levels, which are measured by your works.

Islam doesn't offer _____, _____, and _____. Islam offers _____ but no measure of _____.

Both Judaism and Islam offer a litany of _____, but neither offers _____ with the lawgiver.

Islam allows for atonement, but every man atones for himself. It is a denial of Christ's blood for someone else.

Muslims are stuck in an endless cycle trying to prove their _____.

Every other religion calls men to _____ for their _____. Only in Christianity does _____ die for _____.

Christ's blood means I don't have to be good enough anymore. I don't live by _____. I live by the _____.

Concluding Challenge

We are not, as ambassadors, allowed to _____ the message that God left. It is our job to _____ that message. _____ are at stake.

In confronting the cultures, we must know what we are looking for:
- _____ in what you and others believe.
- _____ is the ability to enter the debate.

The people you are talking to are people for whom _____ died.

CHRISTIAN GROWTH STUDY PLAN

In the Christian Growth Study Plan *When Worldviews Collide: Christians Confronting Culture* is a resource for course credit in the subject area Ministry in the Christian Growth category of plans. To receive credit, read the book; complete the learning activities; attend group sessions; show your work to your pastor, a staff member, or a church leader; then complete the following information. This page may be duplicated. Send the completed page to:

Christian Growth Study Plan; One LifeWay Plaza; Nashville, TN 37234-0117; fax (615) 251-5067; e-mail *cgspnet@lifeway.com*.

For information about the Christian Growth Study Plan, refer to the *Christian Growth Study Plan Catalog*, located online at *www.lifeway. com/cgsp*. If you do not have access to the Internet, contact the Christian Growth Study Plan office, (800) 968-5519, for the specific plan you need for your ministry.

WHEN WORLDVIEWS COLLIDE: CHRISTIANS CONFRONTING CULTURE
COURSE NUMBER: CG-1088

PARTICIPANT INFORMATION

Social Security Number (USA ONLY-optional)	Personal CGSP Number*		Date of Birth (MONTH, DAY, YEAR)
Name (First, Middle, Last)		Home Phone	
Address (Street, Route, or P.O. Box)	City, State, or Province		Zip/Postal Code
Email Address for CGSP use			

Please check appropriate box: ☐ Resource purchased by church ☐ Resource purchased by self ☐ Other

CHURCH INFORMATION

Church Name		
Address (Street, Route, or P.O. Box)	City, State, or Province	Zip/Postal Code

CHANGE REQUEST ONLY

☐ Former Name		
☐ Former Address	City, State, or Province	Zip/Postal Code
☐ Former Church	City, State, or Province	Zip/Postal Code

Signature of Pastor, Conference Leader, or Other Church Leader	Date

*New participants are requested but not required to give SS# and date of birth. Existing participants, please give CGSP# when using SS# for the first time. Thereafter, only one ID# is required. **Mail to:** Christian Growth Study Plan, One LifeWay Plaza, Nashville, TN 37234-0117. Fax: (615)251-5067.

Revised 4-05